CREATE MUSIC
WITH
NOTION

To access online media visit:
www.halleonard.com/mylibrary

Enter Code

8099-1102-6611-6585

quick **PRO**
guides

CREATE MUSIC WITH NOTION

Notation Software for the Busy Musician

George J. Hess

Hal Leonard Books
An Imprint of Hal Leonard Corporation

Published in 2015 by Hal Leonard Books
An Imprint of Hal Leonard Corporation
7777 West Bluemound Road
Milwaukee, WI 53213

Trade Book Division Editorial Offices
33 Plymouth St., Montclair, NJ 07042

Printed in the United States of America

Book design by Adam Fulrath
Book composition by Kristina Rolander

Library of Congress Cataloging-in-Publication Data

Hess, George J. (George John), 1956- author.
 Create music with Notion : notation software for the busy musician / George J. Hess.
    pages cm – (Quick pro guides)
 Each copy of this book will come with a unique code for the reader to access online media files.
 Includes index.
 ISBN 978-1-4803-9615-9
 1. Notion (Computer file) 2. Musical notation–Computer programs. I. Title.
 MT39.H47 2015
 781.3'4536–dc23
                                  2014047286

ISBN 978-1-4803-9615-9

www.halleonardbooks.com

To the women in my life, my wife, Samphoas,
my daughter, Pahna, and my mother, Elizabeth,
for their unconditional love and support

CONTENTS

Chapter 1

Chapter 2

Chapter 3

Chapter 7

Chapter 8

Chapter 9

Chapter 10

Chapter 11

The Jazz Ensemble 119

ACKNOWLEDGMENTS

Writing a book is never a solo endeavor, and there have been many people who have been of great help in getting this out. First, thanks to my wife, Samphoas, without whose support and tolerance of the many hours spent working on it, this would never have been completed. Special thanks to Chris Swaffer, John Mlynczak, and Josh Weesner of PreSonus for their patience in answering my many questions. I'd also like to thank Notion users on the Notion/PreSonus forum, specifically my fellow beta testers who provided many insights into how they use the program. Finally, thanks to my editors at Hal Leonard—Bill Gibson, Jessica Burr, and Iris Bass—for guiding me through the process and to Mike Lawson of TI:ME for initiating the whole thing.

INTRODUCTION

If you are reading this, you have probably already purchased Notion. I'm not sure what inspired you to purchase it. It might have been the price, or perhaps you started out with Progression. Or maybe, like me, you're always looking for a better way. For whatever reason, you've made a good choice.

What sets Notion apart is the ease at which it does almost everything the average musician, professional or amateur, would want to do. You can enter notes, the most common dynamics, the most common articulations, and add repeats and endings all at the same time, using easily remembered shortcuts. When you set up a score and choose instruments, you get great-sounding sampled instruments automatically instead of a cheesy, soft synth. Basically it does with incredible ease 95 percent of what most musicians need.

If you are new to music notation software, Notion is the perfect program for you. You'll appreciate how easy it is to do everything. Everything is in a single window and there are no tools to wade through. All the entry items are found in the palettes and all the functions logically placed in the menus. Virtually everything has a shortcut that's easy to remember. And when you press Play, it will perform your music, not just play it.

For those of you coming from another notation program or a DAW, you'll want to adjust your thinking a little. Most other notation programs are primarily engraving programs. They have features for composing and playback, but the main focus is on the printed page. Notion is different. It's more of a notation-based composition environment and the sound is just as important as the page. But it's not a MIDI program, either. While there are features similar to basic sequencers, playback is controlled by notation entries, not by recording MIDI messages. As someone who used both notation programs and DAWs, this took a little getting used to, but once it became clear, using Notion became much easier.

Notion's extensibility is another plus. The included sample library is enough for many users, but there is also a large library for purchase as add-ons either individually or in bundles. Third-party libraries, such as Vienna Symphonic Library or LA Scoring Strings, are also supported. If you need more extensive mixing or processing, you can use any VST plug-in or ReWire it into your favorite DAW. Notion also supports MusicXML export (and import) for when you need to meet the exacting requirements of publishers.

And then there's Notion for iPad.

How to Use the Book

One of the ironies of reading a how-to book for a software program is that it's a pretty fair bet that the author didn't use a book to learn it. That's not to say we don't crack the manual on occasion, but for many of us, the best way is to dive right in and do something useful. So that's what I'm going to suggest you do as well. Each of the chapters is designed as a stand-alone project. You don't have to do them in order and you don't need to do them all. Look at each project and see which ones most closely resemble what you need to do with Notion. There are step-by-step instructions with shortcut or menu reminders for each project, using the provided example. But I highly recommend you not use my examples. Instead, do something similar that has meaning for you. You'll enjoy the process much more and also will be more likely to remember what you've learned.

Each chapter in the book is written with particular users in mind. But even if you decide not to complete a project, you'll benefit from a quick read-through to learn the new shortcuts and commands.

Chapters 1–3 introduce you to the basics of Notion. Even if you've used notation programs before, I suggest you consider reading these chapters and doing the project in Chapter 2. You'll get a good idea of how to work with Notion and have a solid basis for all the succeeding projects.

Chapters 4–6 are primarily aimed at people new to notation software and pop musicians, with an emphasis on guitar.

Chapters 7–9 are intended for music teachers and students. The chapter on live performance has important implications in both professional and educational settings.

Chapters 10–12 focus on advanced notation topics used by professionals like arrangers and film composers, but teachers will also find many things of use here.

Chapter 13 covers Notion for iPad and the interface differences and special features of this powerful app.

When learning any notation program, the most important thing is to develop a workflow that fits both you and the program. Throughout the book, keep workflow in mind and your goal should be to decide what works best for you. You don't want the software to get in the way of your creativity or efficiency. You'll notice as you progress through the book that the workflow becomes less structured. Notion's design really supports this.

If you choose to use your own examples, undoubtedly you will come to something in your example that isn't in mine. That's okay; it's likely covered in one of the other projects. All of the tools and tasks used in each project are listed in the beginning of the chapter in which they are first introduced and also in the index, both as a tool-based solution and a task-based solution. Of course, other options, such as YouTube or Google, may be even quicker. The Notion forums can also be of help here. And of course, as a last resort, you can always take a peek at the manual.

The Accompanying Online Media

All media examples can be found online—see the front of this book for the URL and your unique access code. Files are organized by chapters. For some chapters there are multiple versions of each example in various file formats. These are indicated by an "Online Media" icon:

For best results, copy the online files to your computer's hard drive. Information about updates and new features released after this book went to press can also be found online at www.halleonard.com/mylibrary.

Chapter 1
THE BASICS

In this chapter, we'll look at the basic features and operation of Notion. It's a good idea to read through the chapter to get a feel for the program. Everything will be covered in later chapters, so you don't need to try to memorize all the details, just try to get a general feel for things.

Setup

Notion will run on any Mac running OSX 10.7 or later and on any Windows computer running Windows 7 or 8. You'll need at least a 2.0 GHz Core Duo processor, 4 GB RAM, and 8 GB of free hard drive space for the samples.

Installation

Create an account at my.presonus.com and use the product key to register your software. You can then download the software and bundled sounds. Installation should begin automatically. If not, double-click "Install Notion" and follow the instructions on the screen. The installation files can also be found on the optional DVD, but you will still need to register your software.

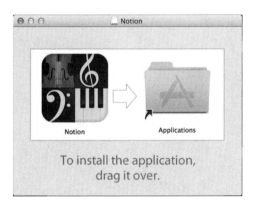

Figure 1-1. Macintosh installation.

Software Activation

The first time you run Notion, you will be asked to activate the software. Notion comes with five activations. If you find you need to move an installed copy, contact tech support and they will provide another install.

Preferences

Preferences are found under the Notion menu (Mac) or the Help menu (Windows).

In the General tab, you can set MIDI input and output options—choose US (alphabetical) or International (numerical) note value shortcuts; set keyboard shortcuts to Notion, Finale, or Sibelius; and set the look of the screen to normal, reverse, or parchment.

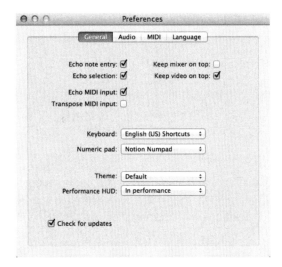

Figure 1-2. General Preferences window.

Audio Preferences

The audio preferences control all of the aspects of Notion's playback.

Figure 1-3. Audio Preferences window.

Audio Devices: Notion selects the default device in your computer setup automatically. However, if you use your computer with different interfaces, you may find you need to select another device and then re-select the default.

Sample rate: Notion's samples can be set to 44.1 KHz (CD-quality) or 48 KHz (video standard). Be sure your audio interface is at the same rate as the sample set or the tuning of the samples will be off. Changing this setting requires you to restart Notion.

Buffer size: The size of the buffer affects sound quality and latency and will depend on your computer and hard drive speed. Smaller values will result in a shorter delay between the time you play a note and the time you hear it. Set the buffer to the smallest value and open one of the demo scores from the Help menu and press the spacebar. If you hear glitches in the playback, then increase buffer size.

Global tuning: The standard tuning frequency has long been A 440; however, many modern orchestras tune to A 442 for a brighter sound. This is a matter of preference.

Enable ReWire: Notion can act as a slave or master when using ReWire to connect to other programs.

Samples Folder: This is where Notion installed its sample set on your computer. You can move the samples anywhere you like and then set the folder here. Also, if you purchase additional sounds for Notion, you may need to re-select the folder for the program to recognize them.

Expansion Sounds

Notion includes a fine sample set that will handle many of your needs. However, for those of you who need additional instruments, a large collection of instruments is available for online purchase from the PreSonus website. Once you download the new samples and install them in the folder, you will also need to activate them. Go to my.presonus.com and enter the product key. You may need to open Notion > Software Activation (Mac) or Help > Software Activation (Windows) and press the Receive Licenses button if Notion hasn't automatically got them.

Other Equipment

Notion works fine on laptops or desktops and doesn't require a numeric keypad. While Notion's interface is primarily in a single window, you may find a second monitor useful for the mixer and for those of you doing video. Laptop users will also find a two-button mouse is well worth the money. Macintosh users may need to go into System Preferences to configure the right-click as the secondary click on their mouse.

> ❶ **TIP:** Beginning with Notion 5, the keypad can be set to use either Finale or Sibelius shortcuts for note values. The options are found in Preferences under the General tab.

MIDI

Notion is specifically setup to work with MIDI keyboards and guitars, but you can connect any MIDI device via USB, a MIDI interface, or wirelessly, using Bluetooth. In my experience, all users will find a MIDI keyboard useful for step-time and real-time entry and you can find suitable ones for as little as $50. I do use a MIDI guitar, too, but for the most part the keyboard is more efficient.

You can connect a MIDI device to Notion for iPad, too, by using either an iPad MIDI interface or the Apple Camera Connection Kit.

All versions of Notion will see and respond to your plug and play MIDI devices automatically. Some older MIDI interfaces may require a software driver to be installed, too. Consult the manual of your device for more information.

Optional Equipment

You can connect your computer directly to headphones or computer speakers, but for the higher-quality sound Notion produces you might want to invest in an audio interface and some near-field monitors. The difference in sound is quite dramatic and worth the investment. After all, you chose Notion as much for the sound as the notation, right?

And a printer goes without saying.

Backup System

There's little more frustrating than working on a project and losing it due to an equipment failure. Notion's auto-save and recovery features are excellent, but nothing survives a crashed hard drive. Make sure you set up a backup system, whether it is an external hard drive or a cloud-based system, such as Dropbox or Google Drive. You'll want this to be automated, because you know the one time you forget is when the crash is most likely.

Interface

With the exception of the mixer and video, Notion uses a single window interface.

Startup Screen

The startup screen provides options to create a new score, open an existing score, or import a MusicXML file, Standard MIDI File (SMF), or Guitar Pro TAB file. A list of recent files and available templates is shown on the bottom half of the window. Click New Score.

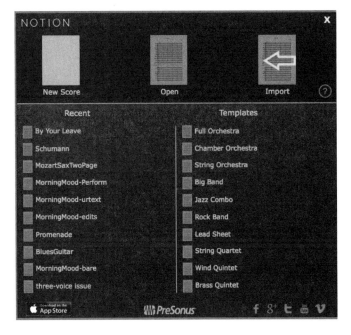

Figure 1-4. The Startup screen.

Score Setup

The top of the Score Setup window displays instruments by categories, while the bottom lets you select the library you are using, including supported third-party external libraries such as Vienna Symphonic Library or Garritan Personal Orchestra. Unsupported VST libraries may also be used but will not respond to expressions, dynamics, and techniques unless a set of external rules is installed or created. You can mix instruments from different libraries in one score. Instruments that are not installed are displayed in *italics*.

Menus

Notion's menus are well organized. The only difference between Macintosh and Windows is in the location of some of the commands. We'll look at commands in more detail as we need them for the projects. For now, just take a look at each one to get a feel for which commands are located in each one.

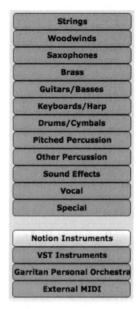
Figure 1-5. The instrument list.

The File menu contains commands for opening, creating, saving, importing, exporting, and printing files.

Figure 1-6. Menus.

The Edit menu contains commands for selecting, copying, and pasting elements.

The View menu controls the display on the screen, zooming, and colors.

The Tools menu contains commands for modifying your music and notation as well as instruments and plug-ins.

The Score menu includes the layout tools for score and parts, plus video and audio setup.

The Window menu lets you choose which interface elements to display.

The Help menu includes the QuickStart Guide and the User Guide, Notion Shortcuts, tutorials, and Demo files.

In this book, menu commands will be displayed as Menu > Menu item; for example, File > New, or File > Rules > Import Rules when a submenu is chosen.

Context Menu

Right-click or Control-click (Mac only) any measure or note to bring up the context menu. This menu contains a selection of most commonly used tools from the main menus. All context menu items except Cut, Copy, and Paste include a submenu.

Palettes

All elements that can be placed in the score are found in the palettes. Select an item from the palette and then click in the score. Most of these items can also be entered using a shortcut that you can see by hovering the cursor over the item. Once again, take a look at each palette now to see what's there.

Figure 1-7. The context menu.

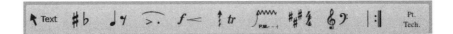

Figure 1-8. The main palette.

They are roughly divided into the following categories:

1. Text
2. Accidentals
3. Notes
4. Articulations and (less common) Dynamics
5. Common Dynamics
6. Traditional Performance Techniques
7. Guitar Performance Techniques
8. Key, Meter, Tempo
9. Clefs and Octaves
10. Repeats and Barlines
11. Instrument Specific Techniques

Throughout the book, items will be identified by <palette number: item>; for example, Palette 3: Quarter-Note, accompanied by the shortcut when applicable.

Toolbar

The Toolbar includes buttons to access to the virtual instruments, the Chord Library, the mixer, and Score Setup mode. These can also be accessed from the Window and Score menu.

Figure 1-9. The Toolbar.

On-Screen Virtual Instruments

Notion includes an on-screen keyboard, fretboard, and drumpad for entering notes. You can also use the fretboard to create custom chord diagrams.

The drum pads are mapped to the correct note on the staff (drum staves use a neutral clef but treat it as a treble clef for note entry with a keyboard or guitar). The Drum Library includes basic drum patterns that can be easily dropped into a measure.

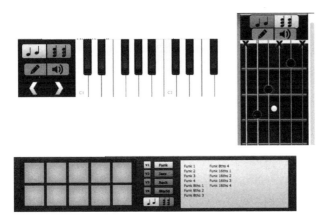

Figure 1-10. The virtual instruments.

All instruments can be set to single note or chord mode. The Pencil button turns on Step-time Recording so notes are entered as you play. In chord mode, press Return/Enter when the chord is complete.

Figure 1-11. Virtual instrument modes.

Mixer

Notion includes an 8-bus, 32-stereo-output mixer with stereo panning and 4 inserts per channel. You can use the built-in effects, Reverb, Compression, and EQ or any VST plug-in. It will also provide channels for external VST or ReWire instruments.

Figure 1-12. The Mixer.

Chord Library

The Chord Library includes chord symbols and optional diagrams. It's important to know that if no diagrams are shown for the chord symbol you have selected, Notion may not play it correctly. In that case you'll either need to notate it or create a custom diagram.

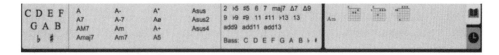

Figure 1-13. The Chord Library.

Transport

The Transport includes Play, Stop, Record, and Rewind buttons, as well as Step-time Record, NTempo Record, Velocity Overdub, and Jump to Rehearsal Letter buttons, along with a counter and audio level meter.

Figure 1-14. The Transport.

Live Performance (NTempo) Mode

Live Performance mode is used in conjunction with an NTempo staff to control playback in real time. This will be covered extensively in Chapter 9.

Figure 1-15. Performance Mode button.

Shortcuts

The mouse is a great invention and it's generally the simplest way to do anything in a computer program. It is also the slowest. Shortcuts in Notion are very easy to remember and are essential if you are to work efficiently. Tooltips are displayed by hovering the mouse over any item in the palettes, if a reminder is needed. Throughout the book, while menu commands and palette items will be indicated, the shortcuts will be provided for any item or tool that has one. Please use them. My recommendation is to never use a menu or palette when it can be avoided.

Shortcuts can be single keys, but often have modifier keys—the Command (⌘) and Option keys on Mac, the Ctrl and Alt keys on Windows, and the Shift key (both)—used in combination with other keys. These will be indicated as ⌘ + <shortcut>, Opt + <shortcut>, etc., or, when modifiers are used together, ⌘-Shift + <shortcut>. Windows shortcuts, when different from Mac shortcuts, will be shown following a slash; for example, ⌘ + T / Ctrl + T or Opt + 3 / Alt + 3.

All shortcuts are lowercase unless Shift is indicated. Many of the shortcuts are immediately obvious—W for whole note, F for *forte*, etc.—but for some the logic may not be immediately clear. For example, Crescendo and Decrescendo shortcuts are the period and comma keys, respectively, but are easily remembered because Shift + period and Shift + comma are the > and < symbols. Similarly, Zoom In and Out is ⌘ + = / Ctrl + = and ⌘ + - / Ctrl + - [dash], but if you look at the keys you'll see plus and minus symbols. There are also a few, like articulations, that aren't as easily recalled, and which you will simply want to memorize.

Many Notion shortcuts have up to eight variants that are accessed by typing the shortcut repeatedly. You don't need to memorize the order, as they will load into the cursor as you type. You'll find this makes them much easier to remember. For example, type Shift + ; (get it? think colon [:]) once for a backward repeat, twice for a forward repeat, and three times for first and second endings.

Essential Shortcuts

Option	Shortcut	Option	Shortcut
Whole note/rest (semibreve)	W	Tie	Shift + T
Half-note/-rest (minim)	H	Repeats/Endings	Shift + ; (colon) (3 variants)
Quarter-note/-rest (crotchet)	Q	Accents	5 (3 variants)
Eighth-note/-rest (quaver)	E	Staccatos	1 (4 variants)
Sixteenth-note/-rest (semiquaver)	S	Tenuto	- (dash)
Triplet (tuplet)	Opt + 3 / Alt + 3	*Fortes*	f, ff, fff, ffff
Dot (double dot)	d (dd)	*Pianos*	p, pp, ppp, pppp
Voice	⌘ + 1–4 / Ctrl + 1–4	Zoom in / Zoom out	In: ⌘ + = / Ctrl + = (equal) Out: ⌘ + - / Ctrl + - (dash)
Enharmonic	Shift + E	Grace note	G

Table 1-1. Essential shortcuts.

This first group should be used at all times. As you can see, most are quite easily recalled.

> **❶ TIP:** Press a note value shortcut once for a note, twice for a rest. Holding the Shift key down after choosing a shortcut also creates a rest.
> Add augmentation dots after selecting a note value and before entering the note.
> Repeat, Accent, Staccato, Forte, and Piano shortcuts cycle through related variants.

Operating Modes

You will always be operating in one of five modes. Being able to switch between them quickly is an important time saver.

Option	Shortcut
Edit mode	Esc
Real-time record	⌘ + R / Ctrl + R
Step-time Record mode	⌘ + E / Ctrl + E
Score Setup	⌘ + T / Ctrl + T
NTempo / Performance mode	Shift + Return/Enter

Table 1-2. More essential shortcuts.

The Esc Key

Most items you choose from the palette, and many tools, will load into the cursor (i.e., the cursor displays the item or tool) and remain there until a new item or edit mode is selected. Use the Esc key to select Edit mode, which clears the cursor and changes it back to the arrow cursor. It's a good habit to press Esc after entering items or using a tool.

More Useful Shortcuts

Once you have command of the essential shortcuts, work on this second tier. They are just as easy to remember, so you should be using them in no time.

Option	Shortcut	Option	Shortcut
Chord tool	Shift + C	Lyrics tool	L
Slur tool	Shift + S	Text tool	K
Clef	C (7 variants)	Sharp	3
Meter tool	Shift + M	Flat	2
Key Signature tool	Shift + K	Natural	4
Barlines	I (3 variants)	Crescendo	, (comma)
Noteheads	X (6 variants)	Decrescendo	. (period)
Duplicate	⌘ + D / Ctrl + D		

Table 1-3. More useful shortcuts.

Once you have those down, try these.

Option	Shortcut	Option	Shortcut
Codas (D.S., D.C., Fine)	7 (8 variants)	Marcatos	6 (4 variants)
Rehearsal letters	Shift + R	Ritard, accel.	R (2 variants)
Fermata, etc.	9 (4 variants)	8va, etc.	Shift + 8 (4 variants)
Beam tool	Shift + B	Tempo marking	Shift + - (dash)

Table 1-4. Other shortcuts.

Instrument Technique Shortcuts

These shortcuts are for techniques specific to certain instruments. Learn the ones you need.

Option	Shortcut	Option	Shortcut
Up/Down bow	U	Bend	B (6 variants)
Harmonics	O	Mute, let ring, slap	M (3 variants)
Gliss portamento	Shift + L	Hammer ons/pull offs	N (3 variants)
Tremolo (measured/ unmeasured)	/ or Shift + /	Slides	\
Pedals	8 (2 variants)	Vibrato/whammy bar	V / Shift + V (4 variants each)
Trill	Shift + ` (~) (4 variants)	Arpeggios	Shift + A (3 variants)

Table 1-5. Instrument technique shortcuts.

Standard Computer Shortcuts

Mac users should be familiar with all of these as they are used for all programs. Windows users see them often but they can vary from program to program.

Command	Shortcut	Command	Shortcut
File Open	⌘ + O / Ctrl + O	Copy	⌘ + C / Ctrl + C
Save file	⌘ + S / Ctrl + S	Cut	⌘ + X / Ctrl + X
Print file	⌘ + P / Ctrl + P	Paste	⌘ + V / Ctrl + V
New file	⌘ + N / Ctrl + N	Undo	⌘ + Z / Ctrl + Z

Table 1-6. Basic computer shortcuts.

Express Entry

Express Entry is a large collection of terms, dynamics, and expressions that can be entered with only a few keystrokes. Some are quite obvious, whereas others are less so. None of these elements will affect playback. To use Express Entry, type ' [apostrophe] followed by the first few letters of the term or dynamic you want. For example, type 'sfz for sforzando, or type 'hal for half-plunger. The list of terms available is found in the manual. The dynamics are easy to remember. For other terms, I recommend you learn the ones you need.

Summary

In this chapter we looked at the basic user interface of Notion. Notion's interface is primarily in one window. All items that are entered into the score are located in palettes. Commands and tools are located in the menus as well as the context menu. Virtually all elements, tools, and commands can be accessed by using shortcuts, which are generally easy to remember. You should have installed the program and connected any external devices you will be using, including a MIDI keyboard. You should know what each of the following are and where they are located.

- Menus
- Context menu
- Palettes
- Toolbar
- Transport
- On-screen instruments
- Chord Library
- Live Performance (NTempo) mode
- Shortcuts
- Express Entry

Chapter 2
GETTING STARTED

We're going to jump right in with the first exercise that I use with every notation class. It will give you a good idea about how to use Notion and some of the power of a notation program. All levels of user will find this one useful, as it will cover most of the basics of Notion and Notion for iPad and will get you up and running quickly.

New Topics	New Shortcuts	
• Creating a score	⌘ + N / Ctrl + N	File > New
• Setting meter		
• Setting key signatures	⌘ + S / Ctrl + S	File > Save
• Delete measures		
• Basic note input	⌘ + C / Ctrl + C	Edit > Copy
• Copy and paste	⌘ + V / Ctrl + V	Edit > Paste
• Transposing		
• Chord symbols	⌘ + X / Ctrl + X	Edit > Cut
• Page layout and formatting	⌘ + D / Ctrl + D	Edit > Duplicate
• Hide meters	⌘ + Z / Ctrl + Z	Edit > Undo
• Hide courtesy signatures	Shift + C	Palette 1: Chord Tool
• Change barlines	W	Palette 3: Whole Note
	Shift + M	Palette 8: Meter
	Shift + K	Palette 8: Key Signatures
	I I	Palette 9: Double Barline

Table 2-1. New skills and shortcuts.

Project Overview

For this simple project, we're going to create a reference sheet that includes all 15 major scales and the primary triads, I, IV, and V, in each key. Shortcut keys, where available, are listed throughout the example. While you don't have to use them just yet, getting in the habit will save you countless hours as you use Notion.

▶ An example of the completed project, "major_scales.pdf," is found in the Chapter 2 folder online at www.halleonard.com/mylibrary. Use this for reference as you complete the project.

Basic Procedure

1. Create a new score.
2. Add a single staff.
3. Change the meter.
4. Set the number of measures per system.
5. Enter notes.
6. Enter chord symbols.
7. Hide the meters.
8. Add double barlines.
9. Duplicate and transpose.
10. Add key signatures.
11. Hide courtesy key signatures.
12. Delete extra measures.
13. Format the score to fit on one page.

Step by Step

Create a New Score

• Open Notion.
• From the startup screen, select New Score.
• If Notion is already open, select File > New (⌘ + N / Ctrl + N).
• From the instrument palettes select Special > Basic Staff.
• Click Exit Score Setup or Esc.

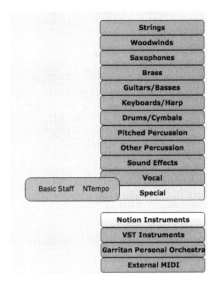

Figure 2-1. Choosing a basic track.

Set the Meter

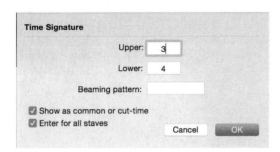

Figure 2-2. The Time Signature dialog window.

- Type Shift + M (Palette 8: Meter).
- Enter 8 for Upper and 1 for Lower.
- Click OK.
- Click to the right of the existing meter in m. 1.
- Type Shift + M (Palette 8: Meter).
- Enter 3 for Upper (1 for Lower will still be there).
- Click OK.
- Click in m. 2.
- Press Esc to clear the cursor.
- Choose File > Save (⌘ + S / Ctrl + S).
- Name the file "Major Scales."

Set Up the Page

By default Notion adjusts the number of measures per line automatically, but for this exercise we need to have two measures in each system. While we're here, we can also turn off staff titles.

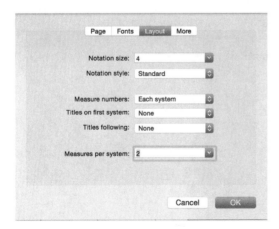

Figure 2-3. Full Score Options: the Layout tab.

- Choose Score > Full Score Options.
- Click the Layout tab.
- Set Measures per system to 2.
- Set Titles on first system to None.
- Set Titles following to None.

Enter Notes

We'll use the simplest point and click method to enter notes. Type W (Palette 3: Whole Note).

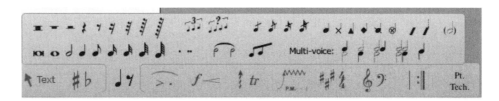

Figure 2-4. The Notes palette (Palette 3).

As shown in the example, enter a C major scale in measure 1. Click in the staff for each note, making sure to click to the right of each note. In measure 2 enter the primary triads. To enter the chords, click the directly above the root note.

Figure 2-5. Example 1.

If you make a mistake, and invariably you will, either choose Edit > Undo (⌘ + Z / Ctrl + Z) or click on the note—it will turn yellow—and use the up or down arrow to change it. When done, press Esc to clear the cursor.

Choose File > Save (⌘ + S / Ctrl + S).

Enter the Chord Symbols

- Select Palette 1: Chord Tool (C7) (Shift + C).
- Click the first chord (you will see a box to show you are over the chord).
- Type C and Return/Enter.
- Click the second chord; type F and Return/Enter.
- Click the third chord; type G7 and Return/Enter.
- Press Esc to clear the cursor.

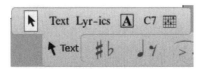

Figure 2-6. The Text palette (Palette 1).

Hide Meters

Hiding meters is not something you will often do, but you can hide almost any attachment, so it's a good thing to know how to do. We will also hide the metronome marking.

- Click the meter in m. 1.
- Shift-click the metronome marking.
- Right-click and choose Attachments > Hide.

Change the Barline

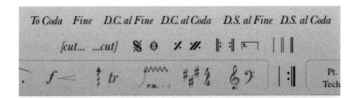

Figure 2-7. The Repeat palette (Palette 10).

There should be a double barline before a key change, so we'll add it now. You should really use the shortcut here.

- Type I I (Palette 10: Double Barline).
- Click in the second measure.
- Press Esc to clear the cursor.
- Choose File > Save (⌘ + S / Ctrl + S).

Copying and Pasting Music, Duplicating, and Transposing

We are now ready to copy and paste this to create the 15 keys. Everything we've done so far will be copied, which will save a lot of time. In most programs, transposing would be done later, and you can certainly wait, but since Notion selects the measures that have been pasted, we'll go ahead and transpose the notes at the same time.

Selecting Measures

The easiest way to select a measure is to double-click it, being sure to avoid clicking an entry. To add to the selection, hold the Shift key down while clicking the last measure of your selection. You can also use the click-drag-enclose method. We will look closely at the different selection methods in chapter 3.

Duplicating

You can always use the standard Edit > Copy (⌘ + C / Ctrl + C) and Edit > Paste (⌘ + V / Ctrl + V) method, but Duplicate combines the two.

- Select the first two measures.
- Right-click anywhere in the highlighted selection.
- Select Edit > Duplicate (⌘ + D / Ctrl + D).

Transposing

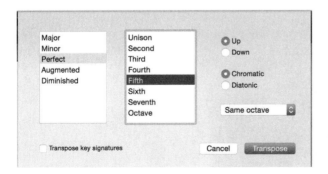

Figure 2-8. The Transpose dialog window.

- Right-click the selection.
- Select Tools > Transpose.
- Set the interval quality to Perfect.

- Set the interval size (see Table 2-2).
- Select Up or Down (see Table 2-2).
- Set the transposition type to Chromatic.
- Check Transpose key signatures.

Use the chart in Table 2-2 to Duplicate and Transpose so we have 15 keys. With the ⌘ + D / Ctrl + D shortcut you don't have to right-click, which will save time. Save the file when you have all 15 keys.

Key	Transposition	Direction
F	Perfect 4th	Up
B♭	Perfect 5th	Down
E♭	Perfect 4th	Up
A♭	Perfect 5th	Down
D♭	Perfect 4th	Up
G♭	Perfect 4th	Up
C♭	Perfect 5th	Down
C♯**	Augmented unison	Up
F♯	Perfect 4th	Up
B	Perfect 5th	Down
E	Perfect 4th	Up
A	Perfect 5th	Down
D	Perfect 4th	Up
G	Perfect 4th	Up

Table 2-2. Transpositions.
**You will need to transpose up an augmented unison twice from C♭ to C♯.

Key Signatures

Now, set the key signatures. We'll follow the circle of fifths counterclockwise, completing all the flat keys before starting on the sharp keys. Key order: C, F, B♭, E♭, A♭, D♭, G♭, C♭, C♯, F♯, B, E, A, D, G.

Setting the Key Signature

Figure 2-9. The Key Signature dialog window.

- Type Shift + K.
- Set Tonic to G and Mode to Major.
- Click OK.
- Click in m. 3.
- Repeat for each key.
- Choose File > Save (⌘ + S / Ctrl + S).

Deleting Measures

There will be an extra couple of measures at the end. To delete them, select them and then choose Edit > Cut (⌘ + X / Ctrl + X) or Edit > Delete. The first option places the cut measures on the clipboard, from which they can be pasted elsewhere. For the most part, Cut, with or without the shortcut, is the better choice.

Note: The Delete/Backspace key will only clear entries, not remove measures.

Hiding the Courtesy Key Signature

Notion 5 now includes Courtesy Time and Key Signatures, which are great additions, but we don't always want them.

- Click each key signature, then right-click it to bring up the context menu.
- Choose Key and Time Signatures > Hide End of System Courtesy.
- Choose File > Save (⌘ + S / Ctrl + S).

Check for Errors

You may notice that Notion chose to simplify some of the chord names by using enharmonic equivalents.

- Double-click the chord symbol "B" in the key of G-flat and type "Cb."
- Double-click the chord symbol "B" in the key of C-flat and type "Cb."
- Double-click the chord symbol "E" in the key of C-flat and type "Fb."
- Double-click the chord symbol "A♭" in the key of C-sharp and type "G#."
- Double-click the chord symbol "D♭" in the key of F-sharp and type "C#."
- Double-click the chord symbol "G♭" in the key of B and type "F#."

Page Layout

We want to get this all on one page, so we need to go back to the Full Score Options and make some adjustments. Choose Score > Full Score Options.

Notion has two top margin settings, one for the first page and another for all other pages. But since we only have one page, we only need adjust the Top, first page setting. Adjust the other settings as shown in Table 2-3, depending on your paper size.

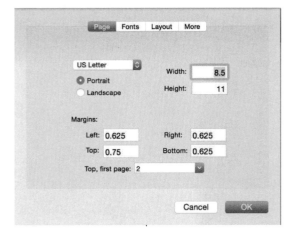

Figure 2-10. Full Score Options: Page settings.

	Tab	US Letter	A4
Top, first page	Page	1.25 inches	1.25 inches
Bottom	Page	0.5 inch	0.625 inch
Notation size	Layout	3.5 pts	4 pts
System break spacing	More	3 spaces	2 spaces

Table 2-3. Layout settings.

Titles, Composers, Etc.

To change the title, double-click it and type "Major Scales and Primary Triads." Delete the composer and date by selecting them and pressing Delete/Backspace.

Choose File > Save (⌘ + S / Ctrl + S).

Next Steps: Details

You may have noticed that as you adjust notes and other items, Notion adjusts the spacing to avoid collisions. It's a feature you'll really come to like. One place it doesn't do this is with chord symbols. The notes of a few of the chords have some ledger lines and they run into the chord symbols. We'll use a hidden command in Notion to adjust the chord symbols slightly.

- Double-click the notes of the chord E♭ in the key of A-flat.
- Type - [dash].
- Double-click the notes of the chord D♭ in the key of G-flat.
- Type - [dash].
- Choose File > Save (⌘ + S / Ctrl + S).

Be careful not to move the chord symbol too much or the staff spacing may be affected too drastically. If that happens, just move the chord symbol a bit closer to the notes.

Summary

This project covered a lot of ground. You now know the basics of using Notion for notation. You should have a good idea how a notation program differs from working with a pencil and how it can help you work faster and more efficiently. Using shortcuts will also save time.

After completing this chapter, you should know how to:

- Create a new score
- Set meter and key signatures
- Enter notes, using the mouse
- Enter chord symbols
- Copy, paste, duplicate, and delete measures
- Adjust the page layout
- Create titles and other headers

Chapter 3
DEVELOPING YOUR WORKFLOW

When learning any software program, the most important thing is to develop a workflow that fits both you and the program. Each program is designed with a workflow in mind that will be most efficient, but you'll want to adapt it to fit the way you like to work. Copyists might work in one way; composers may prefer another. Someone transcribing a solo for saxophone will have a different way of working than will someone creating a TAB arrangement for guitar. Various workflows will be demonstrated throughout the book and your goal should be to decide what works best for you. You want the software to enhance, not interfere with, your creativity and efficiency. Let's look at some of the basic tasks you'll need to consider.

New Topics	New Shortcuts	
• Real-time recording • Step-time recording • Mouse/keyboard entry • Views • Selection methods	⌘ + R / Ctrl + R	Record
	Spacebar	Play/start recording
	H, Q, E, S, T	Palette 3: Note Values/Rests
	2, 3 (#), 4	Palette 2: Flat, Sharp, Natural
	= + <W, H, Q, E, S, T>	Change note value
	Shift + T	Tie
	D	Augmentation dot
	⌘ + = / Ctrl + =	Zoom in
	⌘ + - / Ctrl + - (dash)	Zoom out
	⌘ + A / Ctrl + A	Edit > Select All
	⌘-Shift + A / Ctrl-Shift + A	Edit > Select Part

Table 3-1. New topics and shortcuts.

Entering Music

As with most notation programs, there are three methods of entering notes directly into Notion: real-time recording using a MIDI device; step-time recording using a combination of the computer keyboard and a MIDI or on-screen entry device; and mouse/keyboard entry. Entering notes is what notation software is all about, so it's vital to decide which method works best for you. That said, there will be times that you will use each method. If you are new to notation software, I suggest you complete all the exercises in this chapter. More experienced users who already have a preferred method can skip to that method if they so choose.

Real-Time Recording

"I just want to play and have the software write it down." I've heard people say this countless times over the years. While it would certainly be nice, you'd be surprised at just how complicated it really is. Still, real-time entry can be a useful tool in the right places and Notion is better at it than are most other programs.

So, let's get this out of the way first. Start out by recording something you can play pretty well. It doesn't really matter what it is, but play it the way it should sound; don't think about the notation. The default tempo is 90 bpm (beats per minute), which is probably a good tempo to start with. If you want it faster or slower, double-click the Tempo mark and change the number.

Make sure your MIDI controller is connected to your computer. Click the Record button and then click "Start Recording" or press the spacebar. Press the spacebar or the Esc key when finished.

Figure 3-1. The Transport.

Now try to read it. You'll probably find that it is very hard to read, with lots of smaller note values and rests and maybe a few wrong notes, especially if you are using a MIDI guitar. You likely didn't realize your music was so complicated, but it's an accurate representation of what you played. That's because good notation is really only an approximation of what will actually be played.

So now, let's see what you will work for you. In the online media, you'll find a file, "entry_examples.pdf," with some short examples, each getting progressively a little harder and more complex. Using your MIDI controller, record each one and see what the results are. This will give you a good idea of what will work for you in real-time. MIDI data is a list of performance instructions, so you can record at any tempo that's comfortable and then set the correct tempo for playback later.

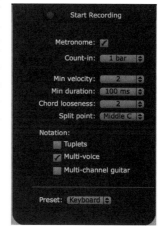

Figure 3-2. Recording options.

To Record Exercises in Real Time

- Connect your MIDI controller to your computer or iPad.
- Create a single instrument score (see page 14).
- Set the meter (Shift + M).
- Set the key (Shift + K).
- Click on the first measure.

- Click the Record button (⌘ + R / Ctrl + R).
- Choose either the keyboard or guitar preset.
- Set the count-off to 2 measures.
- Set Min duration to the smallest note value (see Table 3-2).
- Turn on/off Tuplets, depending on the example.
- Turn on/off Multi-voice, depending on the example.
- Click Start Recording (spacebar).
- Press the spacebar or Esc key when done.

	60 M.M.	96 M.M.	120 M.M.	160 M.M.	200 M.M.
Quarter	1000	625	500	375	300
8th	500	312	250	187	150
16th	250	156	125	98	75
32nd	125	78	62	49	37

Table 3-2. Note values in milliseconds.

Don't feel too bad if this doesn't come out as well as you might have hoped. It can take a lot of practice to play in the strict time that a notation program expects. You really can't play too expressively and you have to be very clean and accurate. With some practice you might find you can do a little better, but in general don't expect different results when you are doing your own project. Also, it's a bit harder with MIDI guitars as there's always a bit of latency involved.

Swing Styles

Notion will notate swing performances correctly. Simply turn off the Tuplets option in the Record dialog box. There is one caveat, though, and that is editing can be quite challenging. If you make any mistakes and have to edit the notes manually, it will be very difficult to get them to playback with the same feel. For that reason, I recommend that you play the music as it's to be written, with even eighths, and use Notion's excellent Swing Control and articulations to apply the feel you want afterward.

When to Use This Method

Real-time recording can still be useful, but it takes some preparation and practice. For the most part, Notion will do a pretty good job of it, but it's important to understand your limitations and that of your MIDI controller. If you don't know your way around a keyboard or guitar pretty well, this method likely won't work for you. If that's the case, I strongly suggest you focus on step-time entry.

For anything other than simple music, real-time recording isn't likely to save you much time. But there is one situation where it is usually the best method to use: when you have the music in your head, but aren't quite sure how to write it down. While it will likely require quite a bit of editing, you will have a basic idea of how it's notated and using Notion's playback as you edit it will help you get it right. We'll look at that in the next chapter.

Mouse/Keyboard Entry

In Chapter 2, we've already seen the most basic entry method, point and click—click on a note value in a palette, then click in the staff. This is fine when you need to add a few notes somewhere, but as a basic method it's much too slow.

However, with a little preparation and by using shortcuts, mouse/keyboard entry can be very efficient. The note value shortcuts are intuitive for those who are familiar with standard American note values, and many of the other shortcuts are easily remembered as well.

The basic shortcuts for note values—W, H, Q, E, S, T—for whole (semibreve) to thirty-second-notes (demisemiquavers), are covered in the Chapter 1. Shortcuts toggle between notes and rests. Press once for note, twice for rest, press again to return to note, and so on. You can also press the Shift key for a rest. Accidentals (2, 3, 4) and augmentation dots (D) are added *before* entering the note. Articulations (1, 5, 6, -) can also be added before entering a note or can be added later in edit mode.

> **❶TIP:** Using the international shortcuts for note values (5–9 corresponding to thirty-second note/demisemiquaver through whole note/semibreve) will interfere with the shortcuts otherwise associated with those keys. For that reason, I suggest international users consider using the US shortcuts or the Finale or Sibelius shortcuts if a keypad is available.

Shortcuts are sticky, meaning they remain selected until you select another value or press Esc. Selecting a new note value will also deselect any articulations.

There's one important exception to this. To clear the Tuplet tool, you must press the shortcut again or Esc. This makes it easy to create tuplets with mixed note values, but can easily lead to mistakes, so get in the habit of canceling your tuplets.

Correcting Mistakes

You will make some mistakes, of course. The simplest thing to do is use the Edit > Undo shortcut, ⌘ + Z / Ctrl + Z, immediately after making a mistake and re-enter the correct note. Undo is unlimited, so you can go back as far as you need to by pressing the shortcut repeatedly. However, sometimes we find our mistakes later on. In that event, do one of the following.

To change the pitch: Press Esc, click on the note, and drag or use the up/down arrow keys to move to the correct pitch. Hold the Shift key while using the arrows to move by half-steps. Holding ⌘-Shift / Ctrl-Shift with the arrow keys will shift the note an octave up or down.

To change the note value: Select the new note value and click directly on the notehead, being careful not to add another note. You can also press Esc, click on the notehead, and press = (the equal sign) and the shortcut for the correct value.

> **❶TIP:** Zoom in (⌘ + = / Ctrl + =) when entering or editing notes with the mouse.

When to Use This Method

The main reason to use this method is when you don't have a MIDI device available. I use this method on planes, trains, buses, anywhere where it's just not convenient to pull out a keyboard or guitar. While it tends to be slower, it affords more flexibility and time to think and experiment than do other methods. For that reason, it's a good method when composing as opposed to just copying.

Another advantage of mouse/keyboard entry is that it is done in Edit mode. This means all shortcuts are available so you can enter not only notes and articulations, but also dynamics, repeats, bar lines, and everything else. This makes it the most like pencil and paper, while offering some of the advantages of a computer-like copy and paste, and playback. If, like Mozart, you conceive of your pieces in their entirety before writing them down, this may be the best method for you. It all comes down to how you like to work. We'll look at that in a later exercise.

Mouse Entry with Shortcuts

Enter this short, single-note example by using the mouse and keyboard shortcuts. For now we'll only worry about entering notes. We'll cover articulations and other entries later.

Figure 3-3. Mouse entry example.

- Open Notion and click New Score or choose File > New.
- Choose Special > Basic Staff.
- Type H (Palette 3: Half-Note), click-in middle C.
- Type E (Palette 3: Eighth-Note), click-in E, D.
- Type Q (Palette 3: Quarter-Note), click-in C.
- Type H (Palette 3: Half-Note), click-in D.
- Type E (Palette 3: Eighth-Note), click-in F, E.
- Type Q (Palette 3: Quarter-Note), click-in D.
- Type D (Palette 3: Augmentation Dot), click-in E.
- Type E (Palette 3: Eighth-Note), click-in G.
- Type Q (Palette 3: Quarter-Note), click-in F, E.
- Type W (Palette 3: Whole Note), click-in D.
- Type QD (Palette 3: Quarter-Note, Augmentation Dot), click-in G.
- Type S (Palette 3: Sixteenth-Note), click-in F, G.
- Type Q (Palette 3: Quarter-Note), click-in F, E.
- Type D (Palette 3: Augmentation Dot), click-in F.
- Type E (Palette 3: Eighth-Note), click-in G.
- Type H (Palette 3: Half-Note), click-in A.
- Type Q (Palette 3: Quarter-Note).
- Type Opt + 3 / Alt + 3 (Palette 3: Triplet), click-in G, A, G, F, E, D.
- Type W (Palette 3: Whole Note), click-in C.

Step-time Recording

Step-time recording uses the shortcuts or palette to select the note value and a MIDI device or on-screen virtual instrument to enter the pitches. Once you start, the Edit marker changes to the Entry marker and advances automatically after each entry. It's best to try to catch and correct any mistakes as soon as they happen, so make sure you take a look once in a while. To delete a note while in step-time mode, press Delete/Backspace or Edit > Undo (⌘ + Z / Ctrl + Z). It is possible to enter too many beats in a measure. If the last note exceeds the number of beats, Notion will not automatically split or shorten the note. Notion cannot automatically reflow notes, either, so if you are off rhythmically, the easiest and fastest thing to do may be to delete the notes and re-enter them.

Keep in mind that the on-screen fretboard is a transposing instrument. That's not a problem for a guitar or bass staff, but notes for most other instruments will be written an octave lower than for guitar notation. You can easily transpose it later.

> **❗TIP:** Avoid playing too legato. Notes must be slightly detached or chords will be created.

When to Use This Method

For most people, step-time recording is the most efficient way to enter notes directly into the program. This is the way most copyists use and it's generally best when you know what you want to write.

The main advantage of step-time recording is that there will be fewer mistakes and you don't have to choose accidentals, though there will occasionally be enharmonic misspellings. The limitation is that you can only add articulations and ties in step-time recording; other shortcuts don't work and must be added later in Edit mode.

Step-time Recording Exercise

Enter this example by using either an on-screen instrument or your MIDI instrument. You can use the score from the mouse entry example or create a new one.

Figure 3-4. Step-time recording example.

- Open Notion and click New Score or choose File > New.
- Choose Special > Basic Staff.
- Type E. Play G, F, E, F.
- Type Q + D. Play G.
- Type E. Play G.
- Type Q + 1. Play F, A.
- Type H. Play D.
- Type Q. Play C + E (together).
- Type 5. Play C + E.
- Type Q. Play D + F.
- Type 5. Play D + F.
- Type H. Play E + G.
- Type Shift + T.
- Type Q + D. Play E + G.
- Type E. Play A, G, F, G.
- Type Q + D. Play A.
- Type E. Play A.
- Type E. Play G, F, E, F.
- Type H. Play G.
- Type Q + 1. Play F, G.
- Type Q + D. Play C + E.
- Type E. Play B + D.
- Type Q. Play C, G.
- Type H. Play E + G + C together.

Other Methods

There are two other ways to get notes into Notion: by importing and by using copy and paste. Notion and Notion for iPad files are interchangeable and can be shared via e-mail, Dropbox, or iTunes. Both programs can import Standard MIDI Files (SMF) and MusicXML files. While many more MIDI files are available for free on the Internet, MusicXML files are the more useful. MIDI files were originally designed to allow users to share files among different sequencers. They are performance-based and contain only MIDI information and generally will require quite a bit of editing. MusicXML files, on the other hand, are notation-based and include most score markings. These generally take much less editing, assuming the original was well done in the first place. Notion and Notion for iPad can also export both file types. We'll look at this in some of the later projects.

Selection Methods

All editing will require that you select an item or section of your score. There are quite a few ways to do this, so once again see which ones suit you best. Each type of selection has a different color associated with it. You need to be in Edit mode to select items. Press Esc.

Basic Selections

- Click anywhere in a measure to position the Edit marker. (Light green)
- Click on any individual item to select it. (Yellow)
- Double-click any measure to select the entire measure. (Gray)
- Triple-click a measure to select that measure for all instruments. (Mac only)
- Choose Edit > Select All (⌘ + A / Ctrl + A) to select all measures of all instruments.
- Choose Edit > Select Part (⌘-Shift + A / Ctrl-Shift + A) to select all measures of the instrument where the Edit marker is located.

Selecting Sections

Click/Shift-click: Use Shift-click to add to any selection. For example, double-click measure 1. Hold the Shift key down and select measure 5. Measures 1–5 will be selected. You can also Shift-click a measure in another staff. All measures for all instruments between the first selected measure and the Shift-clicked measure will be selected.

Click/Command-click (Click/Ctrl-click): Use to add unconnected instruments to a selection. Select the first instrument section and ⌘-click / Ctrl-click another. For example, in a string quartet, double-click a measure in the violin 1 part and ⌘-click / Ctrl-click the cello. The violin 2 and viola staves will not be selected. You can then select additional measures by Shift-clicking.

Click-drag-enclose: This method uses the mouse to select sections of a score. Visualize the selection as a rectangle. Click any corner of the selection rectangle. Hold the mouse button down while dragging the mouse diagonally to the opposite corner of the rectangle.

Finding Your Workflow

The way you create music with Notion will be determined by the project and the way you think about music and, to some extent, by the program. Your workflow will likely evolve over time and vary depending on your mood and inspiration. Most of the time, people don't really think about it, but taking a few minutes to plan will save you time in the long run. It will also help prevent the program from getting in the way of your creativity or efficiency, whichever happens to be most important at the time.

The note entry method you use will go a long way toward determining how you work with the program. If you've chosen the real-time entry method, you will record the notes, edit them, and then add articulations, dynamics, repeats, text, and lyrics.

With step-time recording, you can enter notes, ties, and the most common articulations with the remainder of entries added in Edit mode.

With mouse entry, you are already in Edit mode, so you can enter anything you want in just about any order. This is the most pencil-and-paper-like mode and while it is much slower, when being creative, you may find it to be your preferred method.

What follows are the tasks involved in any project.

Score Setup

This is the first thing to do once you open the software. But you should also consider whether to set up the number of measures and form, include repeats, add rehearsal letters, and so forth. You can always return and do this, but for some projects, you'll find it will save you time to set it up first.

Software or Paper?

Many composers choose to work on paper and use notation software mainly for the engraving. This can be an excellent way to work as it's less likely to interfere with your creativity. But Notion is a little different than most notation programs in that it's faster and more intuitive. Working in Edit mode can be very pencil-and-paper-like. This makes it an excellent composition tool. So, if you really prefer pencil and paper, my suggestion is that you continue to handwrite your notation. However, gradually, try to move to Notion a little sooner. Try getting the basic idea on paper, enter it into Notion, and then use Notion's tools to help realize it.

View

Notion has two basic views: Page view and Continuous view. Which you choose as your primary view is really a matter of personal taste. Page view, which can be set to display by scrolling either across or up and down, has the advantage of looking like a page. It works very well on large screens and has a familiar paperlike feel to it. One drawback is that for larger ensembles, you often see very few measures of the score per screen. Of course, when doing the final page layout, this view is the only option.

Continuous view displays one system and scrolls left to right. On most screens, you'll see more measures per system, and it's particularly useful on laptops. Scrolling with a trackpad or trackball is easy—the Apple Magic Mouse is great here—but it's a little less friendly with the standard two-button mouse with a scroll wheel. And for some, the lack of a page interface is disconcerting.

Regardless of with which view you work, get used to using the Zoom controls (⌘ + = / Ctrl + = and ⌘ + - / Ctrl + -). Zoom in for detail work; zoom out for layout work.

> **❶ TIP:** To scroll horizontally with a standard two-button mouse, hold the Shift key down while moving the scroll wheel.

Articulations, Dynamics, Techniques, Phrases

All of these items affect playback, so you'll want to enter them fairly early in the process. The main decision to make is whether it's important to enter them at the same time as you enter notes. If that's your preference, only mouse/keyboard entry will make sense.

If you decide to enter most of these things after the notes have been entered, then the two basic options are whether to enter by section or instrument and whether to enter everything at the same time or separately based on type (for example, articulations, then dynamics, then techniques, etc.). There are no hard-and-fast rules here. The most important thing, regardless of which way you go, is to use shortcuts as much as possible.

Text

Text can be attached to staves or notes. Chord symbols and lyrics are attached to notes, so they must be entered after all notes have been entered. Techniques, expressions, and tempo markings are attached to the staff. Titles, headers, and footers are attached to the page. Some notations, such as titles and tempos, can be dragged vertically; others, such as chord symbols and dynamics, can be dragged vertically or horizontally; and others, such as techniques, cannot be moved at all.

Lyrics

Lyrics (L) are attached to notes and are generally one of the last things to be entered. In Notion they must be typed directly into the score; unfortunately, you can't cut and paste from your word processor.

Chord Symbols

Chord symbols (Shift + C) can be entered anytime after notes and can be typed directly into the score, or be designed in the Chord Library. A basic collection of diagrams is also included in the library, or you can create your own custom diagrams by using the on-screen fretboard.

Layout

Layout—how the score sits on the page—can be a complex topic. In general, you can do a little bit of it here or there as it suits you, but the final layout cannot be done until all entries have been completed. Notion does a lot of the layout for you automatically, so there are fewer decisions to be made and things are pretty easy to see and work with without having to do a lot of formatting.

Playback

A score can be played at any time; just press the spacebar. Playback always starts from the Edit marker, which turns into the darker green Playback marker during playback and recording. The main decision to make is whether to tweak the performance or not. Tweaking will alter the playback without altering the notation. You can alter the start and release times of notes and the velocities (loudness), and you can also make dynamics slightly stronger or weaker. This will be covered in detail in Chapter 9.

Some Suggested Workflows

Efficient

Use when you are working as a copyist. This includes when you've done most of the composition on paper.
- Plan: locate repeated sections, complex notation problems.
- Score Setup: instruments, keys, meters, pickup measure, repeats.
- Enter notes and basic articulations by using step-time recording, one voice at a time.
- Add all other notation entries, saving slurs for last.
- Text: chords, lyrics, expressions, titles.
- Score layout.
- Parts editing and layout.

Creative

Composing directly in Notion works very well once you get the hang of it. This method will be fairly fluid, moving from one method to another. Most of the time will be spent in Edit mode, which is very similar to working with a pencil and paper. The key to this is using shortcuts. You can easily enter notes, add articulations and dynamics, phrasing, and other techniques, just by selecting shortcuts. You can enter notes with shortcuts and the mouse or quickly jump into Step-time Record mode when you need to work a little faster.

There's no prescribed order to your workflow in this mode. Score setup may be more basic, selecting only instruments, and initial key and meters. Once you are working, you'll of course enter notes first. You can use any method, though I tend to find real-time more of an obstruction here. You can enter as many notes as you want, adding articulations and dynamics along the way when you want.

There's really only one thing that can't be done, and that's entering lyrics and chords before entering notes. For songwriters, this may get in the way a bit.

Explorations

Sometimes, you are just looking for your muse. This is where real-time recording comes into play. Set up a staff, click Record, and start playing. If you like to do this, you will want to create some templates so you can get to work immediately when inspiration strikes. We'll look at this in more depth in the next chapter, but it can work really well when you are looking for an idea, or when you have an idea but aren't sure how to notate it.

Summary

In this chapter we looked at the things that influence the way you work in Notion. Each of the three note-entry methods will suggest different workflows. There's no right or wrong to this; use the one with which you are most comfortable. Selecting items in the score is one of the most important skills; learning the various ways to do this in Notion will be time well spent.

The new concepts covered include:

- Real-time recording
- Mouse/keyboard entry
- Step-time recording
- Selection methods
- Score setup
- Notation entries: articulations, dynamics, phrasing, and techniques
- Different types of text
- Views
- Layout options
- Playback tweaks
- Possible workflows

Chapter **4**
SONGWRITING

There are many ways to write a song. Some people start with lyrics, some with the melody, some with chords, and some with a beat. Trained musicians can often hear a melody in their head and know how it will be notated. Whether you are already comfortable with notation or just starting, one of the best uses for real-time recording is when you are working out a new idea.

Project Overview

In this project, we'll create an eight-measure groove, using the ubiquitous four chords of pop music. Then you'll record your melody in real time using either a MIDI keyboard or guitar. The idea here isn't to create a great accompaniment, but just to provide a framework as quickly as possible for you to work out your melodic ideas. For this example, I'll use a basic rock groove, but feel free to use one of the others or your own idea, if you prefer.

New Topics	New Shortcuts	
• Drum library • Chord library • Chord diagrams • Slash notation • Staff settings	⌘ + E / Ctrl + E	Step-time record
	⌘ + T / Ctrl + T	Score > Score Setup
	⌘-Shift + ↑ / Ctrl-Shift + ↑ (up arrow)	Transpose octave up
	⌘-Shift + ↓ / Ctrl-Shift + ↓ (down arrow)	Transpose octave down

Table 4-1. New skills and shortcuts.

Basic Procedure

1. Create a score for melody instrument and rhythm section.
2. Add a drum beat from the Drum Library.
3. Record a bass line.
4. Record rhythm slashes.
5. Add chord diagrams from the Chord Library.
6. Record your melody.
7. Edit the melody.

Step by Step

Score Setup

Start by creating a score with drums, bass, guitar, and a melody instrument.

- Create a new score (⌘ + N / Ctrl + N).
- Add instruments.
  - electric or acoustic guitar
  - electric or upright bass
  - drum set
  - melody instrument (your choice)

The default placement of the drum set will be above the others as in an orchestra, but here it should be at the bottom. To move it down, click and drag the drum set staff below the bass staff until a gray bar and button appears, then release the mouse button.

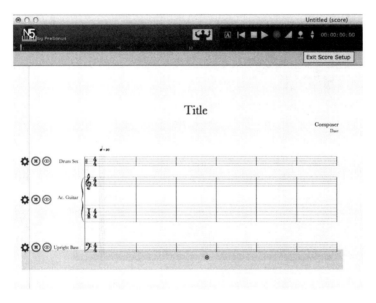

Figure 4-1. Moving a staff.

Hide the TAB Staves

By default, the guitar and bass will have staves for both standard notation and TAB. For this example the TAB is unnecessary, so we'll hide it.

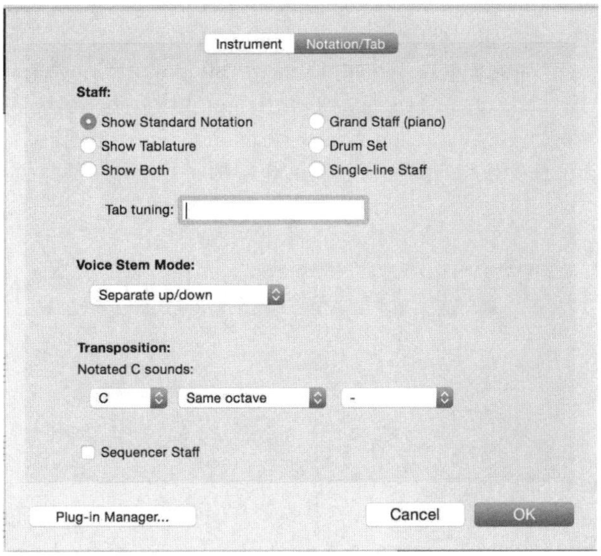

Figure 4-2. Staff options.

- Click the Track Settings button.
- Select the Notation tab.
- Select Show Standard Notation.
- Click OK.
- Click Exit Score Setup.
- Choose File > Save (⌘ + S / Ctrl + S).

Delete Measures

Now delete all but eight measures. Selection methods were covered in the last chapter. In this case, the double-click/Shift-click method works best.

- Select m. 9 to the end.
- Double-click the top staff in m. 9.
- Shift-click the bottom staff of the last measure.
- Select Edit > Cut (⌘ + X / Ctrl + X).

Add a Drum Beat

Notion includes a basic, but very usable, library of rock, funk, jazz, and world drum beats. Most are in 4/4, but a few are in 12/8. The basic patterns can be used individually or chained together to create more complex grooves. Fills should only be used at the end of phrases. We can use one of the patterns for the first four measures of the drum part.

Figure 4-3. The Drum Library.

- Select Rock style, then the Rock 8ths 1 pattern.
- Click in the beginning of the first measure to paste the pattern.
- Right-click and choose Edit > Duplicate (⌘ + D / Ctrl + D) three times.
- Choose File > Save (⌘ + S / Ctrl + S).

Add the Bass Line

The four-chord progression is one that has been used in countless pop songs: C–G–Am–F (or I–V–vi–IV, if you prefer). Some suggested rhythms are shown in Figure 4-4, but you can use any rhythm you like. For a basic rock beat, an eighth-note pattern, using only the chord roots, will work fine. You can use any of the note entry methods, but step-time recording is probably the fastest for a line like this.

Figure 4-4. Suggested bass line rhythms.

- Click the Step-time Record button (⌘ + E / Ctrl + E).
- Type E (Palette 3: Eighth-Note).
- Enter one measure of each of the following notes: C, G, A, F.
- Choose File > Save (⌘ + S / Ctrl + S).

Octave Transposition

Bass is a transposing instrument that sounds an octave below the written note. The starting note should be written one octave below middle C (sounding two octaves below). It doesn't matter whether the other notes are above or below the C, but all three should be in the same octave. If you need to transpose a measure by an octave, double-click it and press ⌘-Shift + ↑↓ / Ctrl-Shift + ↑↓ [up or down arrow key].

The Guitar Part

For the guitar part, we'll start by using Notion's built-in chords from the Chord Library. Chord symbols only play back when slash notation is present, so it's a good idea to enter that first. Some suggested rhythms are in Figure 4-5. You can pick one or write your own.

Figure 4-5. Suggested guitar rhythms with slash notation.

Creating the Slash Notation
- Use either mouse/keyboard entry or step-time recording.
- Enter one measure of the rhythm on middle C. (Don't worry, you won't hear this note.)
- Right-click and choose Edit > Duplicate (⌘ + D / Ctrl + D) three times.
- Select the four measures. Double-click m. 1, Shift-click m. 4.
- Right-Click and select Notes > Show as Rhythm Slash.

Chord Symbols with Diagrams

Chords can be typed directly into the score, but the voice leading from chord to chord usually will not sound very smooth. One way to fix that is to use the chord diagrams included in the Chord Library.

The Chord Library has five sections: Roots, Qualities, Extensions, Bass Notes, and Diagrams. Select a root and then add any other parts of the chord as needed. To make the chords move smoothly, we will have to select diagrams that work together.

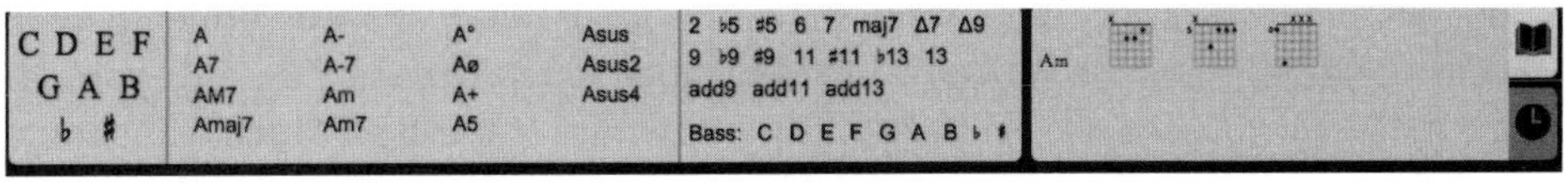

Figure 4-6. The Chord Library.

- Click the Chord Library button in the Toolbar (Window > Show Chord Library).
- Select C as the root.
- Select the first available diagram.
- Click in the guitar staff at the beginning of m. 1.
- Select G as the root.
- Select the first available diagram.
- Click in the guitar staff at the beginning of m. 2.
- Select A as the root.
- Select Am for the quality.
- Select the first available diagram.
- Click in the guitar staff at the beginning of m. 3.
- Select F as the root.
- Select F for the quality.
- Select the first available diagram.
- Click in the guitar staff at the beginning of m. 4.
- Choose File > Save (⌘ + S / Ctrl + S).

Duplicating the Pattern

We now have a four-measure pattern that you may recognize from quite a few well-known songs. For this exercise, the pattern will need to play twice for a total of eight measures, so we need to duplicate all four measures.

- Select the four measures. Use either click/Shift-click or click-drag-enclose.
- Right-click and choose Edit > Duplicate (⌘ + D / Ctrl + D).
- Choose File > Save (⌘ + S / Ctrl + S).

▶ To begin here, open "songwriting.notion" now.

Recording Your Melody

Now you are ready to record. Remember this is a melody, which usually means something that can be sung easily, so don't overplay. You should also be aware that a lot of what you hear singers do are embellishments that are not written down at all. So keep it pretty simple and don't try to be too expressive. Accuracy is the most important thing here. The chord progression is in C major, so your melody can be played using the C major scale (white keys) or C pentatonic (C–D–E–G–A).

- Click at the beginning of m. 1 of your melody instrument.
- Click the Record button (⌘ + R / Ctrl + R).
- Un-tick Metronome.
- Set Count-in to 2 measures.
- Set Preset to Keyboard or Guitar depending on your controller.
- Turn off Multi-voice (if selected).
- Set the minimum duration to 100 ms (>32nd note @ 90 M.M.).
- Click Start Recording (spacebar).

The recording will automatically stop at the end of the song, or you can press spacebar. If you are happy with your take, great. If not, type ⌘ + Z / Ctrl + Z (Edit > Undo) and try again. If you find that you have too many small notes or rests, try a longer minimum duration. If you find there are a lot of notes you didn't intend at all, try increasing the minimum velocity. Continue until you have something that you can live with. It doesn't need to be perfect, just close enough so it can be edited without too much effort.

Editing the Notation

Fixing wrong notes is simple, but the rhythm can pose a challenge. Notion will do a pretty good job of turning your performance into good notation, but playing to a metronome—the drum patterns are just a fancy metronome, really—takes practice. Even if you're a pretty good player, if you haven't done it much, you may find that things didn't turn out as well as you would have liked. You'll have to decide whether editing or recording again is the best. If you decide to edit it, here are some things that might help.

If it looks too complicated, it probably is. Depending on the style, the shortest note or rest in most melodies will be an eighth-note or an eighth-note triplet with perhaps a few sixteenths. Small rests don't belong there. Delete the rests and lengthen or move the notes to cover the space. If there are too many of them, consider recording again with a longer minimum duration.

Find the downbeats. Tap your foot while listening to the recording. Conducting with your hand can help, too. Move all notes you can identify as a downbeats to beat one of the measure.

Find repeating ideas. Good melodies usually have some distinctive ideas. There might be a syncopated note on the + of 4 or a repeating rhythmic idea. Make sure they are notated more or less the same. Listening carefully to how your melody is put together can save a lot of time notating it.

Play back often. You can solo any section by selecting it first and pressing Play (spacebar). Make changes, select it and play it back. Compare it to the original and see if you are closer to what you want.

If you are going to have to do quite a bit of editing, then you might want to duplicate the melody staff. You don't want to edit your original performance, as there's a chance you'll forget what you played. Open Score Setup (⌘ + T / Ctrl + T) and add another staff that uses the same instrument as your melody staff. Select your entire melody track (⌘-Shift + A / Ctrl-Shift + A), then copy (⌘ + C / Ctrl + C) and paste (⌘ + V / Ctrl + V) it to the new staff. Once you have the notation the way you like it, you can delete the original melody staff.

Next Steps: Personal Groove Libraries

The idea behind this example is to get the program out of the way of your creativity and instead use it to foster it. Once you are proficient with Notion, setting up this eight-bar phrase will take less than five minutes. But we can cut it down further. If you tend to compose songs in a particular style, consider creating your own library of grooves that you can copy and paste into your scores.

The Drum Library is a good starting point. Create a score for each of the four styles. Then select each pattern and place it in a measure. Use the Text tool (K) to label each pattern and save the file. Now when you create a new drum pattern, add it to this file, too. Eventually you'll have an extensive library of drum patterns that you can use. You can also do this with bass and guitar, too.

Summary

In this chapter, you learned how to quickly set up a score for a melody and rhythm section, create rhythm section parts by using the chord and drum libraries, and then record a melody in real time and edit it. New concepts included:

- Score setup—multiple instruments
- Staff settings
- Slash notation
- Drum Library grooves
- Built-in chord diagrams
- Notating a melody from a real-time recording
- Templates

Chapter 5
THE LEAD SHEET

A lead sheet is a basic sketch of a song that includes the melody, chord symbols, and lyrics, if applicable. Performers are expected to understand how to interpret it and all musicians work from the same basic lead sheet, though some horn players will prefer one transposed for their instruments, something that's easily done in Notion.

Project Overview

In this project, you'll enter the notes, chords, and lyrics for a 12-bar blues. You'll then format the score using repeats and endings and page layout tools. The lyrics for this song were written by A. A. Chapman in 1871 and are the earliest published reference to the blues in popular song. The music Chapman wrote isn't anything like what we think of as the blues, though, so I took the liberty of using his lyrics with my own music. You can use the provided example, but I would encourage you to expand on the song you wrote in the previous chapter or another you've written previously.

▶ If you are using the provided example, open the online file "AintIGotTheBluesLS.pdf."

New Topics	New Shortcuts	
• Score setup—Jazz font • Pickup measures • Edit tempo markings • Text tempo markings • Simple repeats and endings • Lyrics • Credits • Page layout process	Opt + 3 / Alt + 3	Palette 3: Triplet
	Shift + ;	Palette 9: Backward Repeat
	Shift + ; ;	Palette 9: Forward Repeat
	Shift + ; ; ;	Palette 9: Endings
	L	Palette 1: Lyrics
	L2	Lyrics, verse 2
	Shift + E	Respell enharmonically

Table 5-1. New topics and shortcuts.

Basic Procedure

1. Create a new score with one basic staff.
2. Set up a pickup measure.
3. Set the key.
4. Add a text tempo marking.
5. Enter notes and edit as needed.
6. Enter chord symbols.
7. Enter repeats and endings.
8. Enter lyrics.
9. Enter headers: title, composer, etc.
10. Make final adjustments.
11. Format the page.
12. Proofread and listen.

Step by Step

Create a New Score

The lead sheet uses a single basic staff and the handwritten-style Jazz font. Don't use the lead sheet template in Notion as it's really a grand staff. The form of the blues is in four-bar phrases, so we'll set the score to four measures per line.

- Choose File > New (⌘ + N / Ctrl + N).
- Choose Special > Basic Staff.
- Click Exit Score Setup or press Esc.
- Choose Score > Full Score Options.
- Click the Layout tab.
- Set Notation Style to Jazz.
- Set Measures per system to 4.
- Set Titles on the first system (staff names) to None.
- Set Titles following to None.

Create the Pickup Measure

Right-click the first measure and choose Measure 1 > Pickup Measure. The length of the pickup measure will be set automatically when notes are entered.

Set the Key Signature

- Type Shift + K.
- Select E Major.
- Click in the pickup measure.

Set the Tempo

This a slow blues shuffle. We can enter both text and metronome marking by using the Tempo tool.

- Double-click the tempo marking.
- Type "Slow Blues Shuffle q=72." (Note with the Jazz font, this will look like uppercase Q.)
- Choose File > Save (⌘ + S / Ctrl + S).

Enter the Notes

Whether you are using the provided example or your own song, this is copyist work. Most copyists, myself included, will use step-time recording, as it is the most efficient method and will have the fewest errors. You can also record it in real time, but don't use the mouse to enter notes in this exercise.

Step-time Recording

- Show the virtual guitar or keyboard, if needed.
- Type ⌘ + E / Ctrl + E or click one of the step-time recording buttons.
- Click in the first measure.
- Using the shortcut choose the note value.
- Play the pitch on your MIDI device or click it on the one of the virtual instruments.
- Continue until all notes are entered.

Step-time Entry Shortcuts	
Whole note	W
Half-note	H
Quarter-note	Q
Eighth-note	E
Sixteenth-note	F
Dot	D
Tie	Shift + T
Triplet	Opt + 3 / Alt + 3

Table 5-2. Note values shortcuts.

If you take a look at the melody, you'll notice that there are phrases that are quite similar to one another. In a more complicated piece, we might want to consider using copy/paste and re-pitching the notes. But in a simple piece such as this, it's easier to just enter the notes directly.

Real-Time Recording

You can choose to record in real time, but if you do, be sure to play it using even eighth-notes. If you don't, it will be very difficult to edit later. You can stop and restart anywhere during the recording. The form hasn't been set up yet, so play straight through from the first to the second endings. Add the following settings in the Record dialog box.

Minimum duration	200 ms
Chord looseness	1, single notes
Tuplets	x (tick)

Table 5-3. Record options for real-time recording.

The smallest note value in the melody is a sixteenth-note. At 72 bpm, that will be about 208 ms (1 beat = 60,000/72 or 833 ms), so setting it to the largest value will help Notion get the rhythm right.

Edit the Notes

If you recorded in real time, you probably have at least a few mistakes to correct. If there are a lot of errors, you might want to record it again or consider using Step-time Record. If the rhythms are correct, try re-pitching with a MIDI keyboard. Remember that entering it correctly the first time is generally faster than editing is.

- **To change a pitch:** Select the note and drag or play a new pitch on your entry device.
- **To respell enharmonically:** Type Shift + E and click a note or vice versa.
- **To change a rhythm value:** Select the note(s), type = [equal sign], and then type the note value or shortcut.
- **To delete a note:** Click on the notehead and press Delete/Backspace.

Re-pitching

You can re-pitch existing lines in step-time without changing the note values. Take care not to re-select any note values using shortcuts, as they will cause a rest to appear.

- Click above the first note you want to change.
- Click the Step-time Record button (⌘ + E / Ctrl + E).
- Play the new pitches in order.
- To skip rests, just click the next note.

Tuplets

If any of the tuplets aren't notated correctly, you'll need to enter them manually.

- Delete or edit any wrong notes.
- Mouse-enter the correct notes into the measure. Don't worry if there are too many beats.
- Click-drag-enclose the notes of the triplet.
- Right click and choose Tuplets > Make Tuplet (or select Palette 3: Triplet).

> ❶ **TIP:** To adjust the appearance of a tuplet or create unusual ratios, select any group of tuplets or notes, right-click and choose Tuplets > Custom Tuplets.

Once the notes are entered correctly, save the file (⌘ + S / Ctrl + S).

Enter Chord Symbols

Chord symbols can be typed directly into the score, or you can use the Chord Library to add chord diagrams, if you so choose. Remember, chord symbols do not play without rhythm slashes. See Chapter 4 for more information on entering chords.

Form: Repeats, Endings, Barlines, and Measure Numbers

Most lead sheets will use repeats and often first and second endings. The shortcut Shift + ; creates a repeat—easily remembered, as the two dots of a colon represent the two dots of a repeat sign—cycles through the repeats and endings. Press it once for a backward repeat (:||), twice for a forward repeat (||:), and three times for endings. Always enter the backward repeat before the endings. Endings can be as long as needed; just click in the first measure of the ending. The ending tool will then automatically create brackets for both endings.

- Press Shift + ; for the backward repeat, click in m. 12.
- Press Shift + ; ; (colon, two times) for the forward repeat, click in m. 1.
- Press Shift + ; ; ; (colon, two times) for the endings, click in m. 11.

The form will be just a bit clearer with a double barline at the beginning of the chorus. Type I I and click in m. 14.

The measure numbers now need to be adjusted to allow for the repeated section.

- Choose Score > Full Score Options.
- Select the Layout tab.
- Set Measure Numbers to "Each Measure."
- Click OK.
- Double-click the measure number 13.
- Type 23.

- Choose Score > Full Score Options.
- Select the Layout tab.
- Set Measure Numbers to "Each System."
- Type ⌘ + S / Ctrl + S to save the file.

Enter Lyrics

Lyrics are attached to notes. You can also type one lyric word in an empty measure on beat 1. Generally lyrics are added as one of the last entry items. To enter lyrics, select the Lyric tool, click the first note, type the first word, and press the spacebar to move to the next note. Rests will be skipped automatically. For multi-syllable words, type a dash after the syllable, then press the spacebar. You can select the tool from Palette 1 or just use the shortcut L to get started. For the second verse, type L2. You can have up to nine verses.

To enter lyrics: Type L (or L + <verse number>), click a note, and type the word followed by spacebar.

To enter multi-syllable words: Type - [dash] after the syllable followed by spacebar.

To correct a lyric: Click on the incorrect lyric and re-type.

To delete a lyric: Click on it and press Delete/Backspace.

To copy lyrics: Select the measure with the lyrics to be copied. Right-click and choose Select Special > Select Lyrics. Then choose Edit > Copy (⌘ + C / Ctrl + C).

Enter the following lyrics. Verses 1 and 2 should be before the first and second ending, the chorus after. Make sure you put the first word of verse 2 in the first ending and the last word on verse 2 in the second ending. Enter the chorus in Lyric 1. As this is a blues, the first and second lines of each verse and the chorus are the same. You can copy and paste the lyrics only, if you choose.

"Ain't I Got the Blues" by A. A. Chapman

VERSE 1
This world contains an awful set, and me they so abuse
This world contains an awful set, and me they so abuse
I've got a horrid fit of what the people call the blues

VERSE 2
The sky is blue as indigo, the ground is black as ink
The sky is blue as indigo, the ground is black as ink
I've not a friend in all the world, would you stand me for a drink

CHORUS
Oh ain't I got the blues, my sadness you'll excuse
Oh ain't I got the blues, my sadness you'll excuse
If you knew what it is to have, such a terrible fit of the blues

After the lyrics are entered, type ⌘ + S / Ctrl + S to save the file.

Title and Credits

Page text, such as titles, composers, and so on, is added by choosing Score > Add Title, Header, Footer . . . You are limited to one entry of each type. As such, we'll need to use the Date header for the lyricist. We also want the copyright notice to be centered. We'll need to delete both and create new ones.

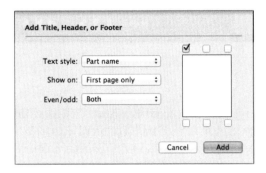

Figure 5-1. The Title, Header, Footer dialog window.

- Double-click the Title and type "Ain't I Got the Blues."
- Double-click Composer and type "Music by George Hess."
- Click Date and press Delete/Backspace.
- Choose Score > Add Title, Header, Footer . . . .
- Set Text Style to Date.
- Tick the top left check box to place it on the top left of the page.
- Click Add.
- Double-click Date and type "Lyrics by A. A. Chapman."
- Click the copyright text in the lower right of the page and press Delete/Backspace.
- Choose Score > Add Title, Header, Footer . . . .
- Set Text Style to Copyright.
- Tick the bottom center check box.
- Click Add.
- Double-click Copyright and add "2014, George J. Hess, all rights reserved" (thank you!).
- When the Font box appears, set the font to TTJazzTextExtended, Size 8.

Adjusting Chord Symbols

There are a couple of things to do before the final page layout. The chord symbols are above the ending brackets, and in most lead sheets they are found beneath them. The chord symbols themselves are a little small. Fortunately these are easy to fix as chord symbols and ending brackets can be moved manually. Click and drag the chord symbols or diagrams down closer to the staff. Don't worry whether they line up perfectly, as we'll fix that next. Then click and drag the ending brackets up above them.

Align the Chord Symbols
- Select (yellow) one chord symbol or diagram.
- Hold the Shift key and select the rest of the symbols on that line.
- Right-click and choose Chords > Align Chord Symbols.

Set the Font Size
- Choose Score > Full Score Options.
- Select the Fonts tab.
- Scroll down to Chord Root.
- Set the size to 18.
- Select Chord label.
- Set the size to 15.
- Type ⌘ + S / Ctrl + S to save the file.

Page Layout

In the first exercise, the layout was pretty easy, as we knew the number of measures per system and each system was the same. This layout will be a little more difficult, as the only thing we know is that it needs to fit on one page. Other than that, our goal is that it is easily read and has a balanced look.

One key to readable copy is to avoid overcrowding and to leave enough white space. Sometimes, smaller print is actually easier to read because of the clarity provided by the white space.

Another thing to consider is the structure and form of the piece. While not a hard-and-fast rule, it's a good idea to try make the phrasing and form as clear as possible. Left and right margins should be equal, but top margins are usually larger than bottom margins. In Notion, the top margin refers to the top staff exclusive of any page text, such as titles and composer credits.

The Layout Process

The first challenge is to get it all on one page. There are three ways to address this. The easiest solution is to reduce the size of the notation. But since lead sheets are often intended for sight-reading, in this case it would be best to leave it as large as possible. Another option is to reduce the white space. We can do this by adjusting margins and adjusting the space between each staff. The third option is to reduce the number of staff systems by moving measures up or down.

Let's start with the third option. There are a total of 26 measures in our song. We earlier set the number of measures per system to four, which translates into six systems with two measures remaining. We should be able to fit this into six systems pretty easily, while still keeping phrasing in mind as much as possible.

Step 1: Endings should either be both entirely in one system or be separated by the first and second ending. Forcing them to be in the same system would make things pretty unbalanced, so the second ending must start a new system. Right-click the first measure of the second ending and choose Measure 23 > Force New System.

Step 2: Right-click the first measure of the first ending and choose Measure 11 > Link to Next Measure. This ensures that the first ending will stay together.

Step 3: This is where the art of layout comes in. There isn't one right answer. The layout should clarify the form as much as possible. As there are 12 total measures in the first three systems, there should be should four per line. But, due to the pickup measure, there are only three full measures in the first line. So, the first thing to do is move measure 4 up to the first system. To do that, right-click measure 3 and choose Measure 3 > Link to Next Measure. Measure 4 will move up to the first system, and notice that measure 8 also moved up from the third system to the second. The system break inserted in the second ending prevented it from moving, so the first three systems now have four measures each, which makes the form very clear.

Step 4: The chorus is a little less clear and there still may also be one or two measures on the second page. Use Link to Next Measure in measure 35. Everything should now be in six systems on one page.

Step 5: This would be acceptable as is, but the form can still be shown a little more clearly. There are a couple of ways to go. With fourteen measures, there can be two systems with five measures and one with four, or six in the fourth system and four in the last two. Let's see how both work. Right-click measure 16 and choose Measure 16 > Link to Next Measure. This will place five measures in systems 4 and 6, and four measures in system 5. Now choose Link to Next Measure in measure 17. This will move measure 18 up and the form should be quite clear now. Choose whichever way you prefer.

Step 6: The last thing is to center the music on the page and move the headers around a little. The default spacing of three spaces works fine, but it's not very well centered on the page. This is because the margin is measured to the top of all entries, including the diagram.

- Choose Score > Full Score Options.
- Select the Page tab, if it isn't already selected.
- Set the Top, first page margin to 1.75 inches.
- Click OK.
- Type ⌘ + S / Ctrl + S to save the file.

Figure 5-2. Page layout options.

Proofreading and Listening

You now have completed your lead sheet. Click in the first measure and press the spacebar to listen your work. If you used your own original composition, listen carefully for any mistakes and go back and fix them. Be critical. Notation is already an inexact science, so it's important that it be as close to what you want as possible.

Next, use the zoom controls and look it over very carefully. Zoom in (⌘ + = / Ctrl + =) and check details such as lyric spelling. Zoom out (⌘ + - / Ctrl + -) and make sure the layout looks good and balanced. When you are satisfied, save the file.

Next Steps: Templates

The lead sheet template in Notion is actually a grand staff for piano using the jazz font. If you are going to write a lot of songs, it would be a good idea to have a template in your personal library.

- Start with the lead sheet we just created.
- Choose File > Save As and name it "Lead Sheet Template."
- Choose Edit > Select All.
- Select Edit > Clear.
- Delete the key signature.
- Set the tempo marking to q=90.
- Delete the lyricist name.
- Change the composer name to your name.
- Change the title to Title.
- Set Measures per system to 4.
- Save.

Protecting the Template

Now that you have your template, you don't want to accidentally make changes to it.

Mac

- Locate the file on your computer.
- Right-click the file and select Get Info.
- Tick "Locked."

Windows

- Locate the file on your computer.
- Right-click the file and choose Properties.
- Tick Read-only next to Attributes.

Summary

The lead sheet is a basic but very important notation style. Since the melody should be clean without a lot of embellishments, it can be entered using either real-time or step-time recording. But in either case, play straight eighth-notes to make editing easier. Chord symbols can be typed directly into the score, but chord diagrams will provide better playback. Setting up templates for style and ensembles that you write for often can save a lot of time. Make sure to include all of the things that don't change and placeholders for some that do.

As we finish this chapter, you should now know about the following:

- The handwritten-style jazz font
- Pickup measures
- Step-time recording
- Note editing
- Simple repeats and endings
- Lyrics
- Layout

Chapter 6
GUITAR
TECHNIQUES

One of Notion's real strengths is guitar notation and playback. Using the on-screen guitar for input makes it easy to get the right notes and fingerings, and the expressive guitar techniques result in some pretty impressive playback of your solos.

Project Overview

In this project, we'll start with the lead sheet from the last chapter and add guitars and bass to create an ensemble. Then we'll add a chorus of guitar solo and finish it off with a repeat of the chorus and a short lead guitar cadenza. The solo is one I played and recorded in a DAW and then transcribed—you can hear the original online: "guitar_solo.wav" and "cadenza.wav." Feel free to use my solo or one of your own. The final score, "blues_chart.pdf," is available online, as is the Notion file of the lead sheet, "bluesLS.notion."

New Topics	New Shortcuts	
• Add instruments • Add measures • Virtual fretboard • TAB editing • Swing control • Slash notation • Articulations • Dynamics • Guitar techniques • Ritards • Fermatas • Fill with rests • Layout • Mixer and effects • Hide attachments	[(bracket)	Forward one entry
	]	Back one entry
	Shift + P (ppppp)	Palette 5: mp
	- (dash)	Palette 4: -
	6	Palette 4: ^ (marcato)
	Shift + S	Palette 4: Slur
	N, NN	Palette 7: Hammer on, Pull off
	B–BBBBB	Palette 7: Bends
	M–MMM	Palette 7: Mute, Let Ring, Slap
	\ , \\	Palette 7: Slide Up/Down
	V–VVVV	Palette 7: Vibrato
	Shift + V–VVVV	Palette 7: Whammy
	Shift + A–AAA	Palette 6: Arpeggios
	7–7777777	Palette 10: Text Repeats (D.S., Coda)
	Shift + GGG	Straight (eighth-notes)
	R, RR	Palette 8: Ritard/accel.
	9	Palette 8: Fermata

Table 6-1. New topics and shortcuts.

Basic Procedure

1. Open the lead sheet from the last chapter (or online).
2. Add two guitars and a bass.
3. Enter the rhythm guitar part using the virtual fretboard, duplicate, and transpose.
4. Enter the bass part using the virtual fretboard, duplicate, and transpose.
5. Enter the lead guitar part.
6. Edit the lead guitar part, notes, and TAB.
7. Edit the rhythm guitar part.
8. Add the coda and D.S. symbols.
9. Add some additional playback controls.
10. Add effects.
11. Apply some finishing touches.
12. Adjust the page layout.

Step by Step

Add Instruments

Open the lead sheet you created in the last chapter. If you used your own song, then use that here, too. You'll also want to create your own solo later on.

- Choose Score > Score Setup (⌘ + T / Ctrl + T).
- Click Guitars/Basses (the tab will remain open).
- Click Electric Guitar twice.
- Click Electric Bass.

Track Setup

We'll need to rename the guitars to avoid confusion. Guitar and bass have both standard notation and TAB staves by default. For this example, leave it that way for the lead guitar, but choose one or the other for the rhythm guitar and bass, whichever one you are most comfortable with.

- Click Score Settings (the Gear icon) for the first Electric Guitar.
- Rename it Lead Guitar, abbreviation Lead.
- Click OK (Return/Enter).
- Click Score Settings for the second Electric Guitar.
- Rename the second guitar as follows: Rhythm Guitar, abbreviation Rhythm.
- Click the Notation/Tab tab.
- Tick either Show Standard Notation or Show Tablature.
- Click Score Settings for the Electric Bass.
- Rename the bass as follows: Bass, abbreviation Bass.
- Click the Notation/Tab tab.
- Tick either Show Standard Notation or Show Tablature.
- Press Esc.
- Type ⌘ + S / Ctrl + S to save the file.

Full Score Options—Measure Numbers and Fonts

Choose Score > Full Score Options and select the Layout tab. Set Notation style to "Jazz" and set Measure numbers to "Each measure." Having measure numbers on each measure will make it easier to keep track of things. Once the piece is done, you can change that.

The Rhythm Guitar Part

You can enter the rhythm guitar with a MIDI keyboard or MIDI guitar by using step-time or real-time recording. But this part can also be entered very quickly using the virtual fretboard. The basic procedure is to select the notes you want on the fretboard and then press Return/Enter. The advantage to using the fretboard is that the TAB will be correct, too.

For playback purposes, which you will see later in this chapter, we need to have a whole beat in the pickup measure, so enter the eighth-rest and eighth-note, using point and click. You'll then need to add the rest before the first melody note, too.

- Type EE (Palette 3: Eighth-Rest).
- Click in m. 0.
- Type E (Palette 3: Eighth-Note).
- Click low E (sixth string, open) between the rest and the barline.
- Type E (Palette 3: Eighth-Rest).
- Click before the first melody note in m. 0.

> **TIP:** Note values shortcuts toggle between notes and rests, so press the shortcut only once to switch between them.

Figure 6-1. The rhythm guitar part.

Now use the fretboard to enter the notes in measures 1 and 2. The basic process is to click the notes on the fretboard and press Return/Enter. Leave the mouse over the fretboard and your left hand over the Return/Enter key and it will be very fast.

- Click the Fretboard button in the Toolbar.
- Click the Chord Mode button.
- Click the Pencil to start Step-time Recording.
- Click the beginning of m. 1.
- Click the top of the sixth string to change the X (mute) to O (open).
- Click the second fret of the fifth string (B).
- Press Return/Enter.
- Click the B again (mutes string). Press Return/Enter (E entered).
- Click the C♯ fourth fret, fifth string. Press Return/Enter (E and C♯ entered on the same beat).
- Click the C♯ again. Press Return/Enter (E entered).
- Click the D fifth fret, fifth string. Press Return/Enter (E and D entered on the same beat).
- Click the D again. Press ⌘ (E entered).
- Click the C♯ fourth fret, fifth string. Press Return/Enter (E and C♯ entered on the same beat).
- Click B second fret, fifth string. Press Return/Enter (E and B entered on the same beat).
- Type Shift + T (Palette 3: Tie).

Measure 2

- Press Return/Enter (E and B entered on the same beat).
- Click the B again (mutes string). Press Return/Enter (E entered).

- Click the C♯ fourth fret, fifth string. Press Return/Enter (E and C♯ entered on the same beat).
- Click the C♯ again. Press Return/Enter (E entered).
- Click the D fifth fret, fifth string. Press Return/Enter (E and D entered on the same beat).
- Click the D again. Press Return/Enter (E entered).

Tuplets

The last notes in measure 2 are a triplet. This can be entered without leaving Step-time Recording mode.

- Type Opt + 3 / Alt + 3 (Palette 3: Triplet).
- Click G third fret, sixth string. Press Return/Enter (G entered, first note of tuplet).
- Click G♯ fourth fret, sixth string. Press Return/Enter (G♯ entered).
- Click G♯ again and B second fret, fifth string. Press Return/Enter (B entered).

The bracket keys [ ] move the entry marker forward or backward one entry. If there are no entries in a measure, the marker will move to the beginning of that measure. Use the] key to move to the beginning of measure 9. Now enter the notes in measures 9–12, using whatever method you prefer. Note that even with a virtual instrument open, you can still enter notes with a MIDI device, if you choose.

Duplicate and Transpose

We can use the same pattern for the first eight measures and transpose the two measures for the A chord.

- Select mm. 1–2.
- Duplicate (⌘ + D / Ctrl + D) them three times to fill mm. 3–8.
- Select mm. 5–6.
- Right-click and choose Tools > Transpose.
- Select Perfect, Fourth, Up.
- Click OK.
- Select mm. 11–12.
- Duplicate (⌘ + D / Ctrl + D) to fill the second ending.
- Type ⌘ + S / Ctrl + S to save the file.

Swing/Shuffle Control

Notion has a great swing/shuffle playback control, but it's well hidden and can only be accessed using a shortcut, Shift + G. This also has multiple variants. Type the shortcut twice to swing only sixteenths—great for funk shuffles; three times for Straight; or four, five, or six times to apply it only to a single staff. For now we want all eighth-notes to swing. This isn't really swing, it's a shuffle, so we need to hide the Swing Control attachment after it's set up. We'll add a descriptive tempo marking later.

Swing Control needs a whole beat to play back correctly, because it's adjusting where the second half of the beat starts. This is the reason we entered a rest in the pickup measure. What makes this such a unique control is that you can easily adjust the placement of the upbeat.

- Type Shift + G.
- Click the rest in the pickup measure of the rhythm guitar part.
- Press Esc.
- Double-click the Swing expression.
- Type a number from 0.00 (straight eighth) to 90.00 (flam). For this song somewhere between 18 and 35 will be good.
- While the word Swing is selected, right-click near, but not on, the word.
- Choose Attachments > Hide.

The Bass Part

Figure 6-2. The bass line.

The bass part is quite simple, playing the root of each chord in eighth-notes. We can do most of this by duplicating and transposing and then editing a couple of notes.

- Select Palette 3: Eighth-Note (E).
- Click the Fretboard icon in the Toolbar, if the fretboard is not already visible.
- Click the pickup measure in the Bass staff (notice the fretboard has four strings now).
- Click the Note icon on the fretboard.
- Click the Pencil (⌘ + E / Ctrl + E) to enter Step-time Recording mode.
- Click the open fourth string E, nine times (once for the pickup and eight times for the first measure).
- Press Esc to exit Step-time Recording mode.
- Duplicate (⌘ + D / Ctrl + D) this measure through m. 11.

Transpose

Measures 5, 6, and 10 should be A (major) chords and measure 9 is a B major chord, so transpose them up a perfect fourth and fifth, respectively.

- Select mm. 5–6 by dragging a box around both measures.
- Right-click and choose Tools > Transpose.
- Set the quality to "Perfect" and the interval to "Fourth."
- Click Transpose (or press Return/Enter).
- Select m. 9 by double-clicking it.
- Right-click and choose Tools > Transpose.
- Set the quality to "Perfect" and the interval to "Fifth."
- Click Transpose (or press Return/Enter).
- Select m. 10 by double-clicking it.
- Right-click and choose Tools > Transpose.
- Set the quality to "Perfect" and the interval to "Fourth."
- Click Transpose (or press Return/Enter).

Measure 12—The Turnaround

When a song repeats its form, the last measure or two before the repeat often employ a turnaround, some combination of chords culminating in a chord that leads back to the beginning. You've already entered this in measure 12 of the rhythm guitar. We'll copy and paste it to the bass and then edit it.

Figure 6-3. Copying the turnaround.

- Click any of the noteheads to be selected.
- Hold the Shift key and click the other noteheads.
- Choose Edit > Copy (⌘ + C / Ctrl + C).
- Double-click the bass staff, m. 12.
- Choose Edit > Paste (⌘ + V / Ctrl + V).

While still selected, use the shortcut ⌘-Shift + ↓ / Ctrl-Shift + ↓ [down arrow key] to transpose it down an octave.

The tie may not have been copied, so if not, enter it now (Shift + T). The last note in the bass should be a half-note. Select the notehead and type "=H" to change it.

Type ⌘ + S / Ctrl + S to save the file.

Performance Editing

Before entering the solo, this might be a good time to do a little work on the performance. We'll add some dynamics, articulations, and guitar techniques.

Dynamics

The dynamics shortcuts "p" and "f" are easily remembered and will provide all the dynamic levels from *pppp* to *ffff*. For this piece, set both bass and guitar to *mp* by typing "p" five times or by typing Shift + P. Click under the first note of each part.

Articulations

The bass is not very distinct, so let's add an articulation to detach the notes slightly. As these are only for playback purposes, we'll then hide the articulations.

- Select (double-click/Shift-click) mm. 1–11.
- Type - [dash] (Palette 4: -).
- Right-click and choose Attachments > Hide.

The downbeat of measures 12 and 24 should be short and accented. Type 6 (Palette 4: ^ [strong accent, or marcato]) and click on each note on beat 1 of measures 12 and 24.

Type ⌘ + S / Ctrl + S to save the file.

Guitar Techniques

Guitar techniques are all found in Palette 7. Except for the triplets, this type of boogie-woogie rhythm guitar part is often muted.

- Select Palette 7: P.M. (M [palm mute]).
- Click the first note of the guitar part.
- Click the last note before the triplet (m. 2, + of 3).
- Repeat through the downbeat of m. 12, avoiding the triplets.

The triplets require a hammer on and a slur to sound correct.

- Select Palette 7: H (hammer on [shortcut N]).
- Click on the second note of each triplet.
- Type Shift + S (Palette 4: Slur).
- Click the first note of each triplet, followed by the second note of each triplet.

Finally, let's add a half-step bend up to the last note of the first ending. We can control the interval and duration of the bend after entering it.

- Select the first bend in Palette 7.
- Click on the last note in m. 12 (G♮).

Figure 6-4. Whole-step bend.

- Click and hold the word "Full."
- Drag down until it reads 1/2, to set the interval.
- Click and hold the handle (small box below 1/2).
- Drag right to set the duration of the bend.

Add Measures

Add measures for the guitar solo and the coda.

Figure 6-5. Half-step bend.

- Type I (Palette 10: Barline).
- Click in the last measure until a total of 16 measures have been added. (There should be 52 measures now.)

Copy/Paste and Duplicate the Rhythm Guitar and Bass

Use the accompaniment for the chorus and the solo, too.

- Select mm. 1–12.
- Type ⌘ + C / Ctrl + C (Edit > Copy).
- Double-click m. 25.
- Type ⌘ + V / Ctrl + V (Edit > Paste).
- While the section just pasted is still selected, type ⌘ + D / Ctrl + D (Edit > Duplicate).
- Type ⌘ + S / Ctrl + S to save the file.

> **❶ TIP:** Even though accompaniment has been added, this can still be displayed as a lead sheet. Open Score Setup (⌘ + T / Ctrl + T) and click the Eye icon for the accompaniment tracks. You now have a lead sheet that plays with rhythm accompaniment.

▶ To begin here, open the file "blues_nosolo.notion."

The Solo Guitar Part

Figure 6-6. The guitar solo.

There are a couple of ways to work with the solo part. One is to enter all the notes (you can also copy the notes from the online file "guitar_solo.notion") and then go back to enter the performance techniques. The other is to work phrase by phrase, adding techniques as you go. It really depends on how much instant gratification you need. Use any note entry method you like. The fretboard isn't quite as fast for single notes, but will still ensure the TAB is correct, so it's a good option. But step-time recording with a MIDI device or even real-time recording will work, too.

Techniques and Articulations

All of the guitar technique shortcuts are located in Palette 7, but the shortcuts, while not as intuitive as others, are still pretty easy to remember with a little effort.

Technique	Shortcut
Bends	B (6 variants)
Palm mute, let ring, slap	M (3 variants)
Hammer ons/pull offs	N (3 variants)
Slides	\ (2 variants)
Vibrato/whammy bar	V / Shift + V (4 variants)
Arpeggios	Shift + A (3 variants)

Table 6-2. Guitar technique shortcuts.

Solo Guitar—Phrase 1

Figure 6-7. Solo guitar first phrase.

One very common technique that Notion doesn't include for guitar (but does include for jazz trumpet) is the scoop. You can hear it on the very first note of the phrase. This is a quick slide into a note from a half-step below. It's faster than a grace note and there's only one attack, usually accented a bit. Fortunately, there's a workaround using a bend. Before getting started, it's a good idea to zoom in a bit (⌘ + = / Ctrl + =) for easier mouse control.

- Drag the note down to D.
- Select Palette 3: # (3) and click the note.

Figure 6-8. TAB example.

The TAB has moved the note to the wrong string, so we'll move it back.

- Press Esc.
- Click and hold the 8 in the TAB.

Figure 6-9. The scoop.

- Drag up to the second string.
- Select Palette 7: B (Bend Up).
- Click on the first note. It will place the default bend of whole step (Full) on the note.
- Press Esc.
- Click on the word "Full" and drag down until it says 1/2 (step).
- Click on the handle (the box) and drag it to the left until it is almost, but not quite, straight. This controls the speed of the bend.

Now add the rest of the techniques and the articulation. There's an accent, a pull off, and a fast vibrato. All three have shortcuts.

- Type 5 (Palette 4: > [accent]).
- Click on the first note.
- Type NN (Palette 7: P [pull off]).
- Click on the D♮.
- Type VV (Palette 7: Fast Vibrato).
- Click on the last note E.
- Press Esc.
- Click on the Vibrato symbol and drag to the right to about beat 4.

Figure 6-10. Whammy vibrato.   Figure 6-11. Vibrato extended.

Select the phrase—click-drag-enclose is a good choice here—and click Play (spacebar) to audition it. If you are satisfied, type ⌘ + S / Ctrl + S to save the file.

Figure 6-12. Solo guitar—phrase 2.

Solo Guitar—Phrase 2

Create the scoop on the first note as in the previous phrase. There are also a couple of slides and a pull off–hammer on combination. They will also need slurs and again there are shortcuts for each.

Figure 6-13. Slides.

- Type \ [backward slash] (Palette 7: Slide Down).
- Click between B and B♭, and again between B♭ and A.

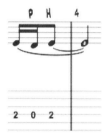

Figure 6-14. Hammer on and pull off.

- Type N (Palette 7: Hammer On).
- Click the E on the + of 4.
- Type NN (Palette 7: Pull Off).
- Click the D before.
    Audition the phrase as before.

Solo Guitar—Phrase 3

Figure 6-15. Solo guitar—phrase 3.

The Let Ring technique is entered in the same manner as slurs, by clicking the first and last note. This will simulate letting the open strings ring while other notes are played. Finish by adding slurs to the two groups of notes.

- Type MM (Palette 7: let ring).
- Click the note B on beat 2, then click the note A on the + of 2.
- Click the note G on beat 4, then click the note E in the next measure.
- Add slurs (Shift + S) to both groups of notes.

- Enter the pull offs and scoop as before.
- Type ⌘ + S / Ctrl + S to save the file.

The last note has a slide up, but there's no note at the other end, giving the impression of just sliding up the string. (In the notation, it appears to slide down, but not in the TAB.)

- Type \ \ (Palette 7: Slide Up).
- Click the last note of the phrase.

Solo Guitar—Phrase 4

Figure 6-16. Solo guitar—phrase 4.

Enter the pull off and let rings as before. The bend on beat 2 of the second measure is actually a whole-step scoop, while the one on the last note is the same basic idea as the last note of the previous phrase, just done a different way. Don't forget the slurs, too.

Solo Guitar—Phrase 5

Figure 6-17. Solo guitar—phrase 5.

Enter this short phrase and use a whammy bar vibrato (VVV) on the last note. As with the fast vibrato, click on the handle and drag it out.

Solo Guitar—Phrase 6

Figure 6-18. Solo guitar—phrase 6.

Once again, when entering the notes, remember to select the note value before typing the triplet shortcut and then to cancel it by typing the shortcut again. Click the Chord tool before entering the last note. The only new articulation is a whammy bar bend (Shift + VV) to be entered between beats 3 and 4 of m. 46.

Type ⌘ + S / Ctrl + S to save the file.

Text Repeats: Signs and Codas

After the solo, the song needs to return to the Chorus and then jump to the ending. Use a D.S. al Coda to jump back: a D.S. sign to indicate where to jump, "To Coda" to jump to the ending, and a Coda sign to signify the ending. All of these are found in Palette 10 and all use the same shortcut "7."

- Type 7 (Palette 10: D.S.).
- Click at the beginning of m. 25.

- Type 77 (Palette 10: Coda).
- Click at the beginning of m. 49.
- Type 777.
- Click the right barline of m. 34.
- Type 77777777 (the 7 key, eight times).
- Click the right barline of m. 48.

Of course, you don't need to memorize these shortcuts. Just type 7 until you see the one you need.

Coda

The coda is a four-bar ending with cadenza-like figure. Start by copying measure 35, all instruments, and pasting it into measure 49. Then copy measure 47 of the lead guitar and paste it into measure 49. Delete the first note of the lead guitar, measure 49, and replace it with a rest (QQ).

You'll need to enter the notes of the cadenza yourself. Use step-time recording or mouse/keyboard entry and try entering the articulations using the shortcuts at the same time as the notes.

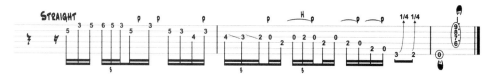

Figure 6-19. Solo guitar—cadenza.

- Press the Chord Mode button and the Step-time Record button.
- Type E (Palette 3: Eighth-Note).
- Play G♯ (first fret, third string) and E (open, first string).
- Press Return/Enter.
- Type E (Palette 3: Eighth-Rest).
- Type SS (Palette 3: Sixteenth-Rest).
- Click the Melody Mode button.
- Type S and 6 (Palette 3: Sixteenth-Note, Palette 4: ^ [strong accent/marcato]).
- Play E (fifth fret, second string).
- Type 5 (Palette 4: > [accent]).
- Play G (third fret, first string) and A (fifth fret, first string).
- Type Opt + 3 / Alt + 3.
- Play B♭ (sixth fret, first string).
- Type S (turn off accent).
- Play A and G (first string).
- Complete the rest of the phrase. Be sure to select Chord Mode for the last notes.
- Enter the pull offs and slides and the two quarter-tone bends.
- Type ⌘ + S / Ctrl + S to save the file.

Coda—Rhythm Guitar and Bass

Add chords in the rhythm guitar and bass to punctuate the lead cadenza.

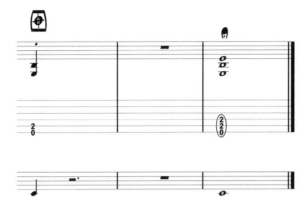

Figure 6-20. Coda—rhythm guitar and bass.

One More Thing

You may notice a clash between the lead and rhythm guitar parts at the end of measure 4. It would be a good idea—though not absolutely necessary, as after all, this is the blues—to delete the triplets in the rhythm part and replace them with eighth-notes. I'll leave it to you to figure out what notes to use. You can also add the pickup note in the voice in measure 48.

Playback: More Swing Control, Ritards, and Fermatas

Sixteenth-notes should be played evenly, but Notion's Swing Control swings both eighths and sixteenths. To change that, Swing Control needs to be canceled.

- Type Shift + GGG (straight).
- Click the rest before the last phrase begins.

Now add a ritard on beat 2 of measure 25. To get ritards (or accelerandos) to play back correctly, you will also have to add a tempo marking sometime after where the ritard is located.

- Type R (Palette 8: *rit.*).
- Click over m. 51, beat 2.
- Set the *rit.* to 50 bpm.
- Type Shift + - [dash] (Palette 8: Metronome Mark).
- Click in the last measure.
- Set the tempo to q=72.
- Right-click near, but not on, the metronome mark.
- Choose Attachments > Hide.
- Type ⌘ + S / Ctrl + S to save the file.

Finally, add the fermatas on the last measure. Fermatas can be set to sustain as long as you like. If the fermata appears below the note, click and drag it above.

- Type 9 (Palette 8: Fermata).
- Click above the last chord in each guitar and the last bass note.
- Press Esc.
- Double-click the fermata in the lead guitar.
- Set the fermata to four quarter-notes.
- Set the fermatas in the rhythm guitar and bass to six quarter-notes.

Finishing Touches

Turn Off Measure Numbers

- Choose Score > Full Score Options.
- Choose the Layout tab.
- Set Measure numbers to Each system.

Double Barlines

Double bars will help players keep track of where they are. Use the shortcut (I I) and click in measures 24, 36, and 48.

Hide Resting Staves

It's common for empty staves to be hidden in a score. In this piece, there's no lead guitar during the verse and chorus and no voice during the solo. These can be hidden. Choose Tools > Hide Resting Staves. This will make the layout easier to deal with.

Type ⌘ + S / Ctrl + S to save the file.

Chord Symbols

Chord symbols aren't necessary on the voice part, but they would be a nice courtesy for the rhythm guitar and bass. You can cut and paste them, but with only three chords, there's a faster way. Don't forget the chord symbols during the solo.

- Type Shift + C (Palette 1: C7 [chord symbols]).
- Click above the first note of m. 1 in the rhythm guitar part.
- Type E7.
- While it's still selected, type ⌘ + C / Ctrl + C (Edit > Copy).
- Press Esc.
- Double-click each measure in which an E7 needs to appear in the bass and rhythm guitar and type ⌘ + V / Ctrl + V (Edit > Paste).
- Repeat with A7 and B7.

You'll need to enter the chords manually in the first ending. Then select all of them (click/Shift-click), and copy and paste them in the appropriate measures.

Figure 6-21. Turnaround chords.

Some chord symbols will need to be adjusted a little to avoid collisions, so go through each chord and adjust it. If there is more than one chord in a line or measure, you may want to align them after adjusting one or more. Select all the chords (only, no notes), right-click, and choose Chords > Align Chord Symbols.

Type ⌘ + S / Ctrl + S to save the file.

Text Tempo Marking

We entered a text description of the style along with the metronome marking in the previous chapter. But often we just want the text. Notion requires a metronome marking for tempo, but it can be hidden by enclosing it in brackets. Double-click the metronome marking and type "Slow Shuffle [q=72]."

Fill with Rests

You don't have to enter rests to fill empty measures or to complete partial measures during note entry. Once all notes are in, choose Edit > Select All (⌘ + A / Ctrl + A), right-click, and choose Tools > Fill with Rests. Now, type ⌘ + S / Ctrl + S to save the file.

Layout

As you've been moving and entering things, you've probably noticed that Notion adjusts the layout to provide space as needed. This can be a real time saver, but at the same time, it means that your control over layout is lessened. It's important to understand that the goal of layout here is to produce clean, readable copy, not publisher-ready scores. Notion's tools for layout are fairly limited and require a bit of trial and error, but in the end there is usually a good solution. Here are the things that will be most useful to adjust. All are found in the Full Score Options dialog window.

Page Margins

The top and bottom margins will help fit more systems on a page or to center the systems. The first page can have a considerably larger margin than the other pages, if needed. It's important to understand that margins are measured from the highest or lowest entry on a staff. Page text, such as titles or page numbers, is not considered.

Left and right margins can change how many measures will fit on a system and can help provide a more balanced look. Unless you have a specific reason, set the left and right margins between 1/2 and 1 inch.

Notation Size

This will affect your layout more than any other setting. It's fine for a score to have smaller notation. Large ensembles should be set to 3.0 points. Parts, on the other hand, should be full size. While the drop-down list suggests values, you can type any size you wish into the box.

System Break Spacing

This is the distance between each system, not each staff. If you have a score with only one staff, this will be the setting to use. Use this to help balance the systems on the page. The drop-down list only goes up to five spaces, but as with size, you can type any number you want.

Font Size

The size of the font for chords and lyrics can have a big effect on spacing. Font size is based on notation size of 4.0. If you reduce the notation size, the text fonts will be reduced accordingly. One way to make a page more readable is to reduce the notation size and increase the text size.

Layout Suggestion

There is no right or wrong answer to the layout for this score. You have to decide what works for you. After some experimenting, these are the settings that I found worked best. Settings not indicated are left at the default setting. Save the file when you are happy with the layout.

Settings		Fonts	
Hide resting staves	On	Lyrics	14 pt
Notation size	3.5	Title	32 pt
System break spacing	8 spaces	Tempo change	16 pt
Measures per system	Automatic	Chord root	16 pt
Top margin, first page	1 inch	Chord label	14 pt

Table 6-3. Suggested page layout settings.

Mixer and Effects

The clean sound for this is fine, but if you'd like to add a little grit to your blues, Notion has you covered with a built-in amp simulator and distortion effect, along with EQ, compressor, limiter, and reverb. You can also use any VST plug-ins you might already have.

- Click the Mixer button in the Toolbar.
- Click the Bus button to hide the Aux tracks.

Each part has its own channel strip with four insert slots for effects, eight sends, solo and mute buttons, stereo pan control, and channel fader. One of the first things you may notice is that the overload indicator is lit for both guitar tracks. This indicates the track has clipped. The Amp Simulator is on by default and it increases the volume, so you'll need to either crank it down or reduce the track volume.

Figure 6-22. Mixer window.

Figure 6-23.
Channel strip.

Amp Simulator

Figure 6-24. The Amp Simulator.

The Amp Simulator has four basic models. For a clean sound, set the gain low and the output high. You can experiment with the resonance and HP filter to create some other sounds. For this example, the following settings were used.

	Lead	Rhythm
Amplifier	1	3
Gain	8.0	7.5
Output	2.5	3.0
Resonance	0.5	0.5
HP Filter	0.0	0.0

Table 6-4. Amp Simulator settings.

Compressor

A compressor is a processor that reduces the overall dynamic range of a signal. Guitarists also use it to increase sustain. The threshold is the volume level at which compression kicks in. The ratio is the amount of input to output signal. For example, with a threshold of –20 dB and a ratio of 3:1, any signal above –20 dB will be reduced by two-thirds (3 dB in, 1 dB out). Gain is then used to increase the overall output of the signal. Attack is the time it takes to reach full compression once the threshold has been reached, and release is the time it takes for the signal to return to normal once the signal goes below the threshold. Reducing dynamic range isn't much of an issue unless you recorded in real time, so it's only used here to increase guitar sustain. Use a medium attack and a long release and increase the gain. The settings used in the example are shown in Figure 6-25.

Figure 6-25. Compressor settings.

EQ

Equalization (EQ) is an essential component of mixing and functions as a separate volume control for each frequency range. The Notion/PreSonus EQ is a four-band parametric EQ, meaning all parameters are adjustable. The top controls indicate the center frequency, while the gain is used to cut or boost that frequency. Q is the width of the effect; a low Q means a smooth slope with a wider band, and high Q is a narrow, focused peak. Generally a small boost or cut with a low Q is enough. Use narrow bands to address any problem frequencies, again something unlikely using samples.

Figure 6-26. The EQ plug-in.

For this example, the lead guitar has a slight boost in the high and mid-range frequencies, coupled with a big (–15 dB) cut of frequencies below 150 Hz. The rhythm guitar has a slight cut in the same mid-range frequencies, a slight boost around 100 Hz, and a big cut above 3 kHz. The bass has a slight boost at 60 Hz and a 2 dB cut at 500 Hz and a big cut at 1000 Hz.

> **TIP:** Be careful with all of these effects, as they are not labeled in any way that would identify to which instrument track it has been inserted. It's very easy to make changes to the wrong effect.

Reverb

Figure 6-27. The Reverb plug-in.

Reverb is used to simulate the sound of a space, whether it be a closet or a cathedral. It can also be used to create depth in a mix. We'll look at that in a later chapter. For now, we'll use a small amount to help unify things. Since we are only using it to help place our ensemble in the same room, it's best inserted onto the Master fader. Set Wet/Dry Mix to 25% and Room Size to 50.

Limiter

The final effect in the chain is the Limiter. The Limiter is used to prevent the overall signal from clipping. Insert it on the Master fader in the last slot and set the threshold to –0.5 dB.

Type ⌘ + S / Ctrl + S to save the file.

Figure 6-28. The Limiter.

Next Steps: TAB and Notation

You may have noticed that when both notation and TAB are displayed, the TAB is limited mainly to string and fret and some techniques. This is because it's assumed that when both are present, the player will be reading the notation for most of the information and the TAB is there to help with fingering. But most players read either TAB or standard notation, not both. So it might be helpful to have a completely notated TAB staff along with a standard notation staff. We can do this with a few tricks.

1. Set Up the Tracks
   - Choose Score > Score Setup (⌘ + T / Ctrl + T or click the Gear icon in the Toolbar).
   - Create an Electric Guitar track (now there are three guitars).
   - Drag the track up under the Lead Guitar track.
   - Click the Track Setup button for the new track.
   - Set Part Name and Abbreviation to "TAB."
   - Click the Notation tab.
   - Tick "Show Tablature."
   - Click OK.
   - Click the Track Setup button for Lead Guitar.
   - Click the Notation tab.
   - Tick "Show Standard Notation."
   - Click OK.
   - Press Esc to exit.
2. Copy the Lead Guitar part to the new track.
   - Click in the Lead Guitar track.
   - Choose Edit > Select Part (⌘-Shift + A / Ctrl-Shift + A).
   - Choose Edit > Copy (⌘ + C / Ctrl + C).
   - Click in m. 0 of the new guitar track.
   - Choose Edit > Paste (⌘ + V / Ctrl + V).
3. Format to look like one instrument.
   - Double-click the lead guitar (any measure).
   - Shift-click the TAB staff.
   - Right-click and choose Staff Groups > Make Barline Group.
   - Select both tracks again.
   - Right-click and choose Staff Groups > Make Brace Group.
4. Mute one track (if both play, the guitar will be twice as loud).
   - Click in the TAB staff.
   - Type ⌘-Shift + A / Ctrl-Shift + A (Edit > Select Part).
   - Right-click and choose Notes > Set as Tacet.

Summary

We covered a lot of ground in this chapter. Entering guitar parts with the fretboard can be particularly useful if you are using TAB staves. The guitar techniques available in Notion are extensive and very effective in creating authentic sounding solos, and the built-in Amp Simulator and other effects processors can make your guitar parts sound even more realistic. Each of the performance techniques has a shortcut assigned, and with shortcut cycling that uses the same key for related techniques, they are easy to remember.

You should now realize that with a little advance planning, copy, paste, and duplicate will save you a lot of time. You should also begin to understand that using shortcuts is the key to working efficiently, no matter what you are doing.

By now, you should also now be in the habit of saving your files. From here on out, there won't be any further reminders. Generally, whenever you complete something you don't want to have to redo, type ⌘ + S / Ctrl + S to save the file.

After completing this chapter you should be familiar with the following:

- Virtual Fretboard
- TAB editing
- Swing Control
- Articulations
- Dynamics
- Guitar performance techniques
- Ritards
- Fermatas
- Fill with rests
- Layout
- Mixer and effects

Chapter 7
PART WRITING
AND ANALYSIS

The four-part chorale is standard material for any music theory class. Students have long been studying the chorale harmonizations of Bach to gather an understanding of tonal harmony and voice leading. This requires not only writing the music, but also analyzing the harmony using Roman numerals and figured bass. Notation programs have made this chore considerably easier. Students can hear what they write—not what they meant to write—and correct mistakes easily.

Transportable files have been a part of the MIDI standard for many years, but they were not ideal for use with notation programs. MIDI files are performance-oriented and require a great deal of editing. A print-based standard, MusicXML, has emerged in recent years. While there are considerably fewer files available in this format than there are for MIDI files, those that are available are very useful.

▶ The complete file "BachChorale.pdf" is available online for reference.

Project Overview

We'll import a MusicXML file of a Bach chorale scored for SATB, condense it, and analyze it with Roman numerals. Beginning in this chapter, shortcuts for many of the common commands and entries will be listed first with the menu or palette locations shown in parentheses. This is to encourage you to think of using the shortcut first.

New Topics	New Shortcuts	
• Importing MusicXML files • Change instruments • Copy/paste voices • Multiple voices • Deleting staves • Meter changes • Roman numeral analysis • Changing fonts • Adding tempo markings • Adding headers • Measure-based formatting	⌘-Shift + I / Ctrl-Shift + I	File > Import
	⌘-Shift + T / Ctrl-Shift + T	Tools > Staff Settings
	⌘ + 1 / Ctrl + 1	Voice 1
	⌘ + 2 / Ctrl + 2	Voice 2
	Shift + - (dash)	Palette 8: Tempo

Table 7-1. New skills and shortcuts.

Basic Procedure

1. Import the file.
2. Change the soprano line to a grand staff.
3. Copy and paste the other voices to the grand staff.
4. Delete the extra staves.
5. Add mid-measure repeats.
6. Enter the analysis.
7. Format the page.

Step by Step

Import the File

- From the startup screen, click the Import icon, or . . .
- Choose File > Import (⌘-Shift + I / Ctrl-Shift + I).
- Select the File "bachchorale.xml" (online).
- Press Return/Enter.

You may notice that Notion thinks the bass part instrument is a transposing double bass. We don't need to worry about that here. It will be fixed automatically in a later step.

Changing Instruments

Four-part writing is usually on a grand staff, so first change the soprano staff instrument to piano.

- Type ⌘-Shift + T / Ctrl-Shift + T.
- Select Keyboards/Harp on the left side and Piano on the right side.
- Press Return/Enter or click OK.

Copying and Pasting Voices

Copy the alto line to voice 2 of the treble (right-hand [r.h.]) staff of the piano part.

- Click in the first measure of the alto staff.
- Type ⌘-Shift + A / Ctrl-Shift + A (Edit > Select Part).
- Type ⌘ + C / Ctrl + C (Edit > Copy).
- Double-click the first measure of the treble (r.h.) staff.
- Right-click and choose Paste Special > Paste into Voice 2.

Now copy the tenor and bass to the bass (left-hand [l.h.]) staff of the piano part.

- Click in the first measure of the tenor staff.
- Type ⌘-Shift + A / Ctrl-Shift + A (Edit > Select Part).
- Type ⌘ + C / Ctrl + C (Edit > Copy).

- Double-click the first measure of the bass (left-hand [l.h.]) staff.
- Type ⌘ + V / Ctrl + V.
- Click in the first measure of the alto staff.
- Type ⌘-Shift + A / Ctrl-Shift + A (Edit > Select Part).
- Type ⌘ + C / Ctrl + C (Edit > Copy).
- Double-click the first measure of the bass (left-hand [l.h.]) staff.
- Right-click and choose Paste Special > Paste into Voice 2.

Deleting Staves

The alto, tenor, and bass staves are no longer needed.
- Type ⌘ + T / Ctrl + T or click the Score Setup button in the Toolbar.
- Click the Delete button next to the alto, tenor, and bass staves.
- Press Esc or click Exit Score Setup.

Mid-Measure Repeats

First and second endings are a relatively modern invention in notation. Prior to that innovation, music with pickup measures that were repeated had a backward repeat placed in the middle of a measure and the forward repeat at the beginning of the piece. We can use a series of hidden meter changes to make the repeat possible.

Delete Repeated Section
- Type I (Palette 10: Barline).
- Click after beat 3, m. 8.
- Click after beat 3, m. 4.
- Press Esc.
- Select what is now mm. 5–9.
- Type ⌘ + X / Ctrl + X (Edit > Cut).

Change Meters
- Type Shift + M (Palette 9: Meter).
- Set Meter to 3/4.
- Click in m. 4.
- Type Shift + M.
- Set Meter to 1/4.
- Click in m. 5.
- Type Shift + M.
- Set Meter to 4/4.
- Click in m. 6.

Add Repeat
- Type Shift + ; [semicolon] (Palette 10: Backward Repeat).
- Click in m. 4.

Hide Meters
- Click each meter change to select it. (Yellow)
- Right-click and choose Attachments > Hide.

Link Measures

It's a good idea to keep the three measures together.
- Click/Right-click m. 4.
- Choose Measure 4 > Link to next measure.
- Click/Right-click m. 5.
- Choose Measure 5 > Link to next measure.

Roman Numeral Analysis

Notion does not include a font for Roman numeral analysis and figured bass, but it does support third-party fonts. The Sicilian Numerals font by Ronald Caltabiano is one of the more complete analysis fonts, is very easy to use, and includes a very generous site license that allows teachers to distribute the font to students. A demo version (SicilianNumeralsDemo.sit) is included online.

Installing the Font

Mac:

- Double-click the file "SicilianNumeralsDemo.sit."
- Drag the font to the MacHD/Library/Fonts folder.

Windows 7:

- Double-click "SicilianNumeralsDemo.zip."
- Double-click SICINDRG (TrueType font file).
- Click Install.

Entering the Analysis

The analysis is shown in Figure 7-1. The Lyric tool is used to attach the analysis to the bass line. Entering the analysis as lyrics instead of text ensures that the analysis stays in place when the score is formatted.

Figure 7-1. The Roman numeral analysis.

Most of the analysis is entered using the I and V keys and the number keys 2, 4, 6, and 7. For major chords use the uppercase I and V; for minor and diminished, use lowercase. Holding the Shift key while typing a number enters it as superscript; typing a number without the Shift key enters it as subscript. The font automatically places the figured bass numbers in line vertically.

For example, to create a I six-four symbol:

   Type: Shift + I, Shift + 6, 4 (no spaces between).
   Result: I_{4}^{6}.

To create the $\mathrm{vii}^{\circ6}_{5}/\mathrm{V}$:

   Type: v, i, i, o, Shift + 6, 5, /, Shift + V.

Symbol	Type	Windows ALT Codes
I	Shift + I	
V	Shift + V	
i	i	
v	v	
Figured bass upper	Shift + <number>	
Figured bass lower	<number>	
o	o (letter, not zero)	
ø	Opt + O (letter, not zero)	ALT 0175
N	Opt-Shift + N	ALT 0247
/	/	
G	Shift + G	
It	Opt-Shift + I	ALT 0246
F	Shift + F	
+	Shift + =	

Table 7-2. Commonly used analysis symbols.

To enter the analysis:
- Type L (Palette 1: Lyr-ics).
- Click the first bass note.
- Type the analysis (Shift + V).
- Press the spacebar to move to the next note.
- Continue through the first ending as shown.

The Sicilian Numerals font is capable of quite a bit more. Feel free to complete the analysis for the rest of the chorale on your own. It'll be good practice for theory students.

Modulations and Pivot Chords
While there are no modulations in the previous example, there certainly will be examples that do have them. For pivot chords, enter the analysis for the new key in verse 2 (L2), then return to verse 1 (L) and continue in the new key.

Entering the Key
It's customary to indicate the key of the analysis. We'll use the Text tool for this.
- Type K or select Text from the palette.
- Place the cursor immediately before the first chord.
- Click and type "g:" [g + Shift + ;].
- Press Esc.
- Click and drag the text in front of the first Roman numeral.
- Increase the size of the text to 12.

You may need to drag the text again to get it to line up. This may take a few tries.

Playback Editing

Metronome Marking

Notion automatically adds a metronome mark to new scores. Because this was imported, there is no tempo indicated. Notion's default tempo of 90 M.M. might be a little quick for this piece, so let's add a tempo marking to slow it down a little.

- Select Palette 8: Metronome Mark (Shift + - [dash]).
- Click above the pickup measure.
- Set the tempo to "q=72."

Fermata Timing

Most of the fermatas were already included, but there was one missing. We can also control their effect on playback. Type 9 (Palette 8: Fermata) and click above the note (G) on measure 4, beat 3. Now adjust the timing of each fermata.

- Double-click each fermata.
- Enter "1 quarter notes" (the duration added by the fermata).
- For the last fermata enter "3 quarter notes."

Title and Composer

- Double-click the title and type "Ach Gott, vom Himmel sieh' darein."
- Choose Score > Add Title, Header, Footer.
- Set Text Style to Composer/Lyricist.
- Press Return/Enter or click Add.
- Type "Arr. J. S. Bach."

Layout

With eleven measures plus a pickup measure, this should fit nicely on four systems. Start by setting the number of measures in each system.

- Choose Score > Full Score Options.
- Click the Layout tab.
- Set Measures per system to 3.

Notion counted the pickup measure and counted the mid-measure repeat as two measures. This leaves one measure in the last system. Let's try to move it up to the previous system.

- Right-click the next to last measure.
- Select Measure 11 > Link to Next Measure.

  Next, adjust the spacing between systems to better center the music on the page.
- Choose Score > Full Score Options.
- Click the More tab.
- Type 8 into the System Break Spacing field.

Next Steps: Assignments and Worksheet Templates

While this exercise is very student-oriented, teachers can also use Notion to create worksheets and assignments. Any font can be used with the Lyric tool. There are some very useful free fonts, including Scale Degrees and Figured Bass fonts available from Matthew Hindson (http://hindson.com.au/info/). If you plan on doing a lot of assignments, it would be a good idea to create a template. Let's create a template for 15 short four-part writing examples.

- Create a new score with a single piano staff.
- Select m. 16 to the end and delete (⌘ + X / Ctrl + X).
- Choose Score > Full Score Options.
- Select the Page tab.
- Set the Top, first page margin to 1.5.
- Select the Fonts tab.
- Set Lyrics to Sicilian Numerals 16 pt.
- Select the Layout tab.
- Set Notation Size to 5. (Type this, as it's not one of the options in the drop-down list.)
- Set Measure Numbers to "Each measure."
- Set Titles on first system to "None."
- Set Titles following to "None."
- Set Measures per system to "3."
- Select the More tab.
- Set System break spacing to six spaces.
- Click OK.

Customizing Suggestions
- Click and drag the header text, Title, Composer, and Date, to the desired location.
- Double-click Title and type "Assignment."
- Double-click Composer and type "Name" followed by underscores.
- Double-click Date and add underscores.
- Type I I (Palette 10: Double Barline) and click in each measure.
- Type K (Palette 1: Text) and add key names at each barline. These are a little tricky to add. Be sure to click right below the barlines. Once entered, they are easily edited by double-clicking or easily deleted using Edit > Clear Special.

  Don't forget to lock the template. (See Chapter 5, Next Steps.)

Summary

Being able to do homework or create worksheets is an essential part of music education. Notion handles this easily and the playback quality makes it easier to aurally proofread your work. The addition of free and inexpensive third-party fonts extends the capability even further. Other than the shortcuts used by Sicilian Numerals, we didn't need many new shortcuts, so hopefully they were all familiar to you.

Students who completed this chapter should now be able to do their homework and also know how to do the following:
- Import MusicXML files
- Paste into voices
- Change meter
- Hide meters
- Change fonts
- Add Roman numeral analysis
- Add tempo markings
- Add headers
- Format measures

Chapter **8**
THE ENSEMBLE ARRANGEMENT

One of the best ways to get notes into Notion is by importing files: Standard MIDI Files, MusicXML files, or Guitar Pro TAB files. Thousands of these files are available for free on the Internet at such sites as Classical Archives (classicalarchives.com), IMSLP (imslp.org), Guitar Pro Tabs (guitarprotabs.org), and Ultimate Guitar (ultimateguitar.com). You can search for a specific piece or browse by performer, composer, or genre.

Each of these types of files will present its own challenges. We looked at MusicXML files in the last chapter. These should be the most accurate as these are specifically designed to share files between notation programs. They should, in theory at least, include pretty much everything and require only some format editing. The reality is that MusicXML is an evolving standard, and as such a lot of things have not yet been standardized. Nonetheless, for printed notation, MusicXML should be your first choice, particularly for public-domain classical works.

Standard MIDI Files (SMF) were designed to share files among sequencers/DAWs. They only include MIDI messages: notes, velocities, program changes, and other data plus some text such as titles and instrument names. These will generally require more editing than MusicXML files. For example, MIDI uses numbers for pitches, so enharmonic notes, such as C-sharp and D-flat, are the same. Similarly, MIDI can't differentiate between a staccato eighth-note and a sixteenth-note and will notate it as the latter. Nonetheless, MIDI files can save time and there are far more of them available than there are MusicXML files. So let's see how to make use of this great resource for repertoire.

Project Overview

Whether it's due to budget issues, unusual instrumentation, or some other reason, finding quality repertoire can be a challenge for school music programs. In this project, we'll import a Standard MIDI File of a public-domain work, String Quartet No. 1 in G, movement 3, by Mozart, and create an arrangement of it for young wind players. Depending on the length and complexity of the piece, you can have a complete arrangement with parts in under an hour. Additional files are provided for this example, if you want to skip some steps.

New Topics	New Shortcuts	
• Importing MIDI files	1, 11, 111	Palette 4: Staccatos
• Sequencer tracks • Enharmonics	5–5555	Palette 4: Accents
• Clear velocities	- (dash)	Palette 4: Tenuto
• Note editing • Trills	6–666	Palette 4: Strong Accents
• Voice colors • Check range	f–fffff	Palette 5: Fortes
• Dynamics	p–ppppp	Palette 5: Pianos
• Articulations • Rehearsal letters	Shift + f	Palette 5: Mezzo Forte
• Advanced layout	Shift + p	Palette 5: Mezzo Piano
• Dynamic parts	Shift + , (<)	Palette 5: Crescendo
	Shift + . (>)	Palette 5: Decrescendo
	77777	Palette 10: D.C. al Fine
	7777	Palette 10: Fine

Table 8-1. New topics and shortcuts.

Basic Procedure

1. Import a Standard MIDI File and convert it to notation.
2. Clear all velocities.
3. Delete repeated sections and replace with repeat signs.
4. Set the key signatures.
5. Edit notes—enharmonics, trills, swap voices.
6. Fill in missing rests.
7. Change the instrumentation.
8. Check the range.
9. Change the key.
10. Exchange parts for variety and to create smoother lines for wind players.
11. Add dynamics, articulations, and phrasing.
12. Add rehearsal letters.
13. Format the score.
14. Format the parts.

Step by Step

Import the File

- Choose File > Import (⌘-Shift + I / Ctrl-Shift + I) *or* click Import at the top of the Startup screen.
- Locate the file "WAM_Minuet.mid" (online).
- Click OK (Return/Enter).

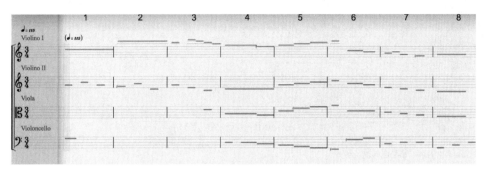

Figure 8-1. Sequencer tracks.

Notion imports the file into sequencer tracks that are similar to piano-roll views found in most DAWs. Notes can be edited in this mode and you can see how it will be performed, but for this exercise we can just go straight to converting to notation.

- Choose Edit > Select All (⌘ + A / Ctrl + A).
- Choose Tools > Convert to Notation.

Now play the file. You'll probably notice that it's not very musical, particularly the dynamics. You can probably guess what dynamics were used when the file was created, but because this is a MIDI file, dynamics are only numbers and aren't displayed. While we have everything selected, this is a good time to remove the velocities from the MIDI notes and let Notion's playback take over.

Clear Velocities
- Right-click inside the selection.
- Choose Tools > Clear Velocities.
- Press Play. You'll notice that it's immediately more musical.

Set the Key Signatures
The minuet is in G major. Often this is included in the MIDI file, but not in this case.
- Type Shift + K (Palette 9: Key Signatures).
- Set Key to G Major.
- Click OK. The key signature is loaded into the cursor.
- Click in m. 1 *after* the meter.

The trio section modulates to C major. Repeat this process and change the key to C major in measure 29.

Set the Form
This is a standard-form minuet and trio. The overall form is a rounded binary with each section repeated. We can shorten the score considerably by using repeats. Notion will handle the playback easily.

Delete the repeated sections as shown in Table 8-2. Note that the measure numbers listed have been adjusted to account for the deleted measures. After deleting measures 9–16, you will keep the new measures 9–28. It will also be a good idea to add the repeats while you do this. Use the shortcut Shift + ; [semicolon]. Type the shortcut once for backward repeats and twice for forward repeats.

	Keep	Delete	:ll	ll:
A	1–8	9–16	8	9
B	9–28	29–48	28	29
C	29–36	37–44	36	37
D	37–52	53–end	53	

Table 8-2. Form and repeats setup.

- Select mm. 9–16.
- Type ⌘ + X / Ctrl + X (Edit > Cut).
- Type Shift + ; (Palette 10: Backward Repeat), click in m. 8.
- Type Shift + ; ; (Palette 10: Forward Repeat), click in m. 9.
- Press Esc.

  Repeat this process with the other repeated sections to complete the form.
- Delete mm. 29–48. Place a backward repeat in m. 28 and a forward repeat in m. 29.
- Delete mm. 37–44. Place a backward repeat in m. 36 and a forward repeat in m. 37.
- Place a backward repeat in m. 51. Delete m. 52 to the end.

  Note: These are not the original measure numbers. They change as we delete measures.

  We need a D.C. al Fine and a Fine to complete the form.
- Type 77777 (the 7 key, five times) until D.C. al Fine is loaded in the cursor.
- Click the final barline.
- Type 7 until Fine is loaded in the cursor.
- Click over beat 2 of m. 28.

▶ To begin here, open the file "Mozart_form.notion."

Note Editing

MIDI files are seldom clean and perfect. I could have cleaned this one up for you, but thought it best to leave it as is. Notion does a good job of guessing the correct notation, but there are enharmonic misspellings and other errors. These are very common in MIDI files, so let's fix them now.

Enharmonics

In this example, the enharmonic errors are located in measures 12–20. Locate the first enharmonic error in the violins in measure 13. Use the shortcut Shift + E to select the enharmonic tool, then click the note (or select the note and then type the shortcut).

The section from measure 37 to the end has quite a few problems that are easily fixed. Here is where we see Notion's editing power. By using shortcuts in Edit mode, it's very easy to switch from one task to another. So, rather than handle each problem separately across the score, we can work measure by measure.

Measure 40—Trills

Trills are written out in many MIDI files. It will sound correct, but it's not good notation practice. Let's change them to a quarter-note with a trill. Notion will, of course, play the trill correctly.

Figure 8-2. Selecting the trill notes.

- Drag a box around all but the last note of the trill, as shown in Figure 8-2.
- Press the Delete/Backspace key.
- Click the notehead of the remaining note.
- Type = + Q to change it to a quarter-note.
- Type Shift + `. (Note: This is the tilde, ~, which looks like a trill.)
- Click above the trilled note.
- Click again on the next note.

Measures 41 and 42

All the notes should be in voice 1. To locate the voice errors, it's helpful to turn on Voice Colors. To do this, choose View > Show Voice Colors.

The first voice problems are the low Gs in measures 41 and 42 in the violins. The notes are doubled in the viola and cello, so delete them. Then delete the rests in voice 2 in those measures.

Measure 43

The notes on beat two of the violins are very large leaps for wind players. Swapping them will make for smoother lines that will be easier to play.

- Click-drag the A in violin 1 up to E.
- Click-drag the E in violin 2 down to A.
- Select (click-drag-enclose) the notes on beat two in both violins.
- Right-click and choose Tools > Swap Voices. The notes move to voice 1 and replace the rests.
- Select and delete the rests in voice 2.
- Fix the trill on beat 3 in violin 1 as before.

Figure 8-3. Measure 43 edited.

Measures 44 and 45

There are notes in voice 2 in both violins and the cello and a trill in the cello.

- Select beats 2 and 3 in violin 1.
- Right-click and choose Tools > Swap Voices.
- Select beat 3 through m. 45 in violin 1.
- Right-click and choose Tools > Swap Voices.

- Select beats 1 and 2 in the cello.
- Right-click and choose Tools > Swap Voices.
- Fix the trill in the cello.
- Select m. 44 in all parts.
- Right-click and choose Select Special > Select Voice 2.
- Press Delete/Backspace.

Finish by swapping the notes in voice 2 in measures 46, 51, and 52 and deleting the remaining rests in voice 2.

Measures 37–42

The double stops in the viola won't be playable by wind instruments, so they will be split between viola and cello. Using copy, paste, and duplicate will save some time.

- Select mm. 37 and 38 in the viola part.
- Press Delete to clear the measures.
- Double-click m. 39 of the viola part to select it.
- Copy the measure (⌘ + C / Ctrl + C).
- Paste it into m. 37 (⌘ + V / Ctrl + V).
- While the measure is still selected, type ⌘-Shift + ↑ / Ctrl-Shift + ↑ [up arrow key] to transpose it up an octave.
- Type ⌘ + D / Ctrl + D to duplicate the measure in m. 38.
- Now paste (⌘ + V / Ctrl + V) the same measure into m. 37 of the cello. (It should still be in the Clipboard.)
- While the measure is still selected, transpose it down an octave. Type ⌘-Shift + ↓ / Ctrl-Shift + ↓ [down arrow key].
- Type ⌘ + D / Ctrl + D three times to duplicate the measure in mm. 38–41.

Fill with Rests

You have probably noticed that Notion doesn't automatically fill measures with rests when importing a MIDI file. Fixing it is simple.

- Type ⌘ + A / Ctrl + A (Edit > Select All).
- Right-click anywhere in the selection.
- Choose Tools > Fill with Rests.

Change Instruments

Now we are ready to choose instruments for the saxophone quartet.

- Select the first violin staff.
- Choose Tools > Staff Settings (⌘-Shift + T / Ctrl-Shift + T).
- Choose Soprano Saxophone (or an instrument of your choosing).
- Repeat with the other staves until you have your desired ensemble.

▶ Open "Mozart_saxes.notion" to begin here.

Transpose and Change Key

Transposing this down a little to an easier key will make it more playable. As we already set key signatures in measures 1 and 29, the Transpose Tool can change them all at once.

- Type ⌘ + A / Ctrl + A (Edit > Select All).
- Right-click and Select Tools > Transpose.
- Choose Major, Third, Down, Chromatic, Same Octave.
- Tick the Transpose Key Signatures checkbox.

Check Ranges

To make sure that the ranges work for saxes, choose View > Show Out of Range Color. It turns out that there are now a couple of out-of-range notes in the baritone sax in measure 36 and again in measure 52. Click each and drag it up one octave to F.

An Arranging Decision

For variety, let's give the melody to the alto sax for the first part of the Trio section. The eight measures from measures 29–36 are virtually identical to the last eight measures (45–52), so this will be quite simple. This will be done very quickly using the shortcuts rather than menu or context menu commands.

- Select mm. 29–36 in the soprano sax part.
- Type ⌘ + C / Ctrl + C (Edit > Copy).
- Double-click m. 45 in the alto sax part.
- Type ⌘ + V / Ctrl + V (Edit > Paste).
- Select mm. 29–36 in the alto sax part.
- Type ⌘ + C / Ctrl + C (Edit > Copy).
- Double-click m. 45 in the soprano sax part.
- Type ⌘ + V / Ctrl + V (Edit > Paste).
- Select mm. 45–52 of both soprano and alto sax parts.
- Double-click m. 45 in the soprano part; Shift-click m. 52 in the alto part.
- Type ⌘ + C / Ctrl + C (Edit > Copy).
- Double-click m. 29 of the soprano sax part.
- Type ⌘ + V / Ctrl + V (Edit > Paste).

Dynamics, Articulation, Phrasing

Mozart included some dynamics and articulations in his quartet, but it's a good idea to be a little more specific for a young ensemble. All articulations, basic dynamics, crescendo/decrescendo, and even slurs—basically anything that can be entered with a shortcut—affect playback.

Once again, in Edit mode you can either add each element separately—articulations first, then dynamics, then phrasing, and so forth—or use the shortcuts and do it measure by measure. This is really a matter of personal preference. Entering all of one element saves some time by not having to switch tools, but Notion's shortcuts make this so easy to do all at once that you'll find it worth the effort and it will seem a little more holistic. My preference is to first enter everything that has a shortcut and then handle anything else after that.

Editing Shortcuts

All elements can be chosen from the palettes, but as we've seen the shortcuts are the best option. These shortcuts are very intuitive and easy to remember. Articulation and dynamic shortcuts cycle through related options. For example, for *forte*, type f. For *fortissimo*, type ff, and so on. Articulations are similar. The basic articulation is set by typing the shortcut once, and less common variations are set by typing the same shortcut two or more times.

Enter Articulations, Dynamics, and Slurs

- **To add articulations to a single note:** Select the shortcut and then click the note.
- **To add the same articulation to multiple notes:** Select the notes first and then select the shortcut.
- **To add dynamics:** Select the shortcut and click in the score, taking note as to which staff is highlighted.

- **To enter slurs:** Select the slur tool; click the first note, then the last note of the phrase. Don't hold the mouse button down between clicks.

Articulations	Shortcuts	Dynamics	Shortcuts
Staccatos	1, 11, 111	*Forte*s	f, ff, fff, ffff
Accents	5, 55, 555, 5555	*Piano*s	p, pp, ppp, pppp
Tenuto	- (dash)	*Mezzo forte*	Shift + F
Strong accents	6, 66, 666, 6666	*Mezzo piano*	Shift + P
Slurs	Shift + S	Crescendo/decrescendo	< >

Table 8-3. Articulations and dynamics shortcuts.

Crescendos/Decrescendos

Crescendos and decrescendos (hairpins) can be added anywhere in the same manner as slurs; select the shortcut (< or >), click the note where it starts, then click the note where it ends. Placement is automatic. But to affect playback, a dynamic must first be placed on the starting and ending note. These dynamics can be hidden, once the hairpin has been created, by right-clicking the individual dynamic and choosing Attachments > Hide from the context menu.

Now enter the articulations, dynamics, and phrasing for the entire piece. Use the file "Mozart_complete.pdf" as a guide.

> **🛈 TIP:** When notes on the same beat have the same articulation on adjacent staves, you can select all at once by using a click-drag-enclose selection and typing the shortcut. This works even when some staves within the selection have rests.

Express Entry

This is a special set of shortcuts that can be added by first typing '(apostrophe) followed by the shortcut. While it can be used for most techniques and expressions, it works particularly well with dynamics as they are easily remembered. Most shortcuts entered in this manner will not affect playback or may not playback correctly. For example, the *fp* dynamic will be interpreted as *forte* only. We'll look at some workarounds for this in the next chapter.

- Type 'fp (apostrophe + f + p).
- Click in m. 9 of the soprano, alto, and baritone parts.

Rehearsal Letters

Rehearsal letters (Shift + R) are found in palette 1. Select the tool with the shortcut and click in measure 9, measure 29, and measure 37. The letter will be automatically incremented. You can also click on any of the rehearsal letters and change them if you prefer another style. Be sure to press Esc when done.

▶ Open "Mozart_edited.notion" to begin here.

Formatting: Three-Page Layout

It's important to understand that while Notion is notation-based, it's not a professional engraving program. Notion will easily produce excellent readable and functional printouts suitable for performance, teaching, and so on. However, there are limits to the layout controls it provides and it can't produce scores that will conform to a publisher's strict requirements.

The challenge here is to use the page as efficiently as possible, while making the score clearly readable with a balanced look throughout. Try to use most of each page, but as long as at least half of the page is used, it will be fine. Do try to avoid the single system on the final page. Above all, we don't want to waste too much time on layout.

The score can fit on two or three pages, depending upon the size of the notation. Let's take a look at both.

For this type of work, I recommend that you set the view to Pages Across. The first step is to zoom out (⌘ + - / Ctrl + - [dash]) until you can see an entire page. Most of the tools you need are found under Score > Full Score Options, with the rest located in the context menu. Here are the settings you have to work with. They can be done in any order and you'll likely have to adjust some of them more than once.

Now take a look at the score. There's quite a bit to not like about this: the difference in top and bottom margins, the inconsistent look of each page, and the form isn't very clear.

The decisions we have to make start with how many pages we want. With eight systems, it would seem that a three-page score would be the way to go at this size.

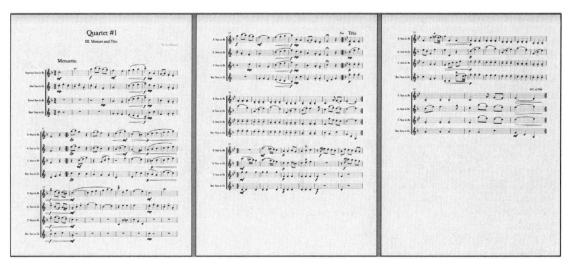

Figure 8-4. Score pre-layout.

For the three-page layout, we'll want three systems per page for a total of nine. With 52 measures, 6 measures per system should be about right.

1. Measures per System

- Choose Score > Full Score Options.
- Select the Layout tab.
- Set Measures per system to 6.

You may notice the drop-down list only goes to 5. No matter, you can type any value in the boxes in this dialog box.

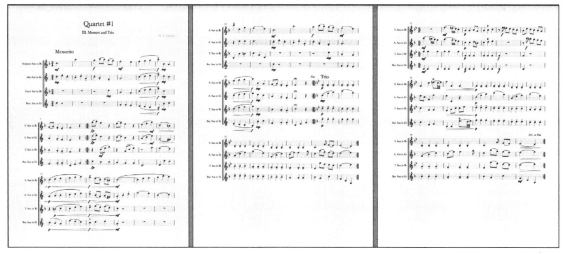

Figure 8-5. Measures per system adjusted.

2. Page Margins

That went a long way toward fixing our layout, but the top and bottom margins are still too unequal. Let's fix them now.

- Choose Score > Full Score Options.
- Select the Page tab.
- Set the top margin and the Top, first page margin to 1.5 inches.

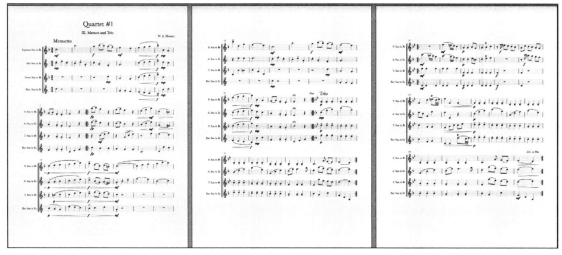

Figure 8-6. Margins adjusted.

3. System and Staff Spacing

This is pretty good and we could chose to just leave it like this. But opening it up just a bit will improve the readability a bit.

- Choose Score > Full Score Options.
- Select the More tab.
- Set Staff spacing to 1.5 spaces.
- Set System break spacing to 5 spaces.

We now have a very functional and readable score that would work for any conductor. While we did it in only three simple steps, don't forget you may have to try a few different settings before you get it just right.

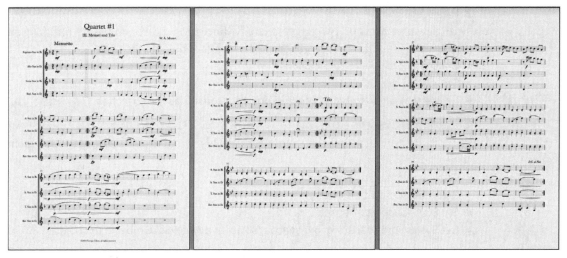

Figure 8-7. Staff and system spacing adjusted.

Formatting: Two-Page Layout

The two-page layout is a little more challenging. We'll start with the three-page layout and make adjustments from there.

1. Notation Size

While we want the font to be as large as possible, be aware that a smaller font size may actually be more readable due to a better balance between print and white space.

Start by reducing the notation size to 3.5 points. While you're at it, reset Measures per system.

- Choose Score > Full Score Options.
- Select the Layout tab.
- Set Notation size to 3.5.
- Set Measures per system to Automatic.

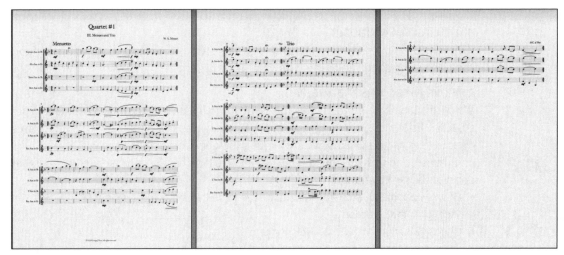

Figure 8-8. Notation size reduced, measures per system automatic.

This looks better but leaves us with the dreading "hanging" system, a single system on the last page. You might be tempted to reduce the notation size to 3 points and that is an option, but there's a better way.

2. Page Margins

To fit seven systems on two pages, there will need to be three on page 1 and four on page 2. Increasing the top margin on the first page should do the trick.

- Choose Score > Full Score Options.
- Select the Page tab.
- Set the top margin to 1 inch and the Top, first page margin to 2.5 inches.

3. Staff and System Spacing

With the smaller notation size, our spaces are also smaller, so we can increase them some.

- Choose Score > Full Score Options.
- Select the More tab.
- Set Staff spacing to 1 space.
- Set System break spacing to 3 spaces (select and type this number in the box).

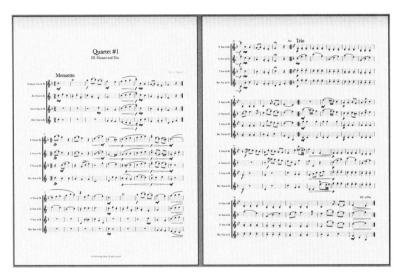

Figure 8-9. Spacing adjusted.

4. Titles and Composer

Adjusting the margins has no effect on page text. Click and drag the titles and composer information and drag it down as shown.

5. Move Measures Manually

While this looks pretty good, it would be better to balance the number of measures per system a little more. Some have as many as nine or as few as five. With 52 measures divided over seven systems, we are looking for 7 or 8 measures in each.

In the second system, the last measure is part of the next phrase. Let's move that down to the next system.

- Double-click m. 16. (You don't actually have to do this, but it makes it easier.)
- Right-click the selection.
- Choose Measure 16 > Force New System.

That makes the first page work nicely. On the second page, the last system only has five measures, so let's work backward to balance this out better.

- Double-click m. 46.
- Right-click the selection.
- Choose Measure 46 > Force New System.

This leaves five measures in the third system. Repeat the same process in measures 39 and 32. Now there are seven measures per system and we have a very balanced-looking score.

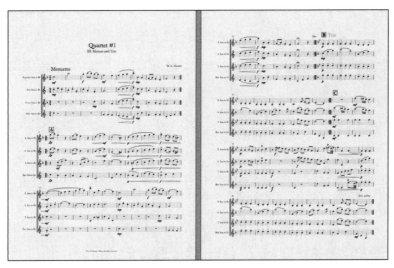

Figure 8-10. The finished two-page layout.

Parts

Notion automatically creates parts that are almost immediately usable. You'll need to add titles, composers, and part names and may need to do a bit of formatting on the page, but that's all. Anything entered in the score is included in the part.

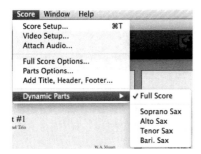

Figure 8-11. Opening parts.

Part Names

If you add one part name manually, Notion will then apply names to all parts automatically.

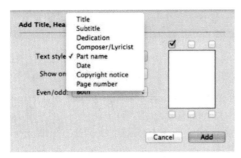

Figure 8-12. Adding part names.

- Choose Score > Add Title, Header, Footer . . . .
- Set Text style to "Part Name."
- Tick the top left box.
- Click Add.

Changing the Font

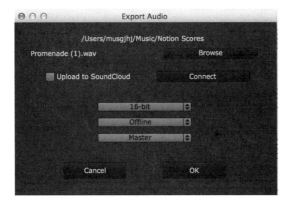

Figure 8-13. The font dialog window.

You can globally change fonts for any text style in Full Score Options, but for text that is only likely to appear once, it's just as easy to change it individually. Click on any text in the score to display the font selection box. Use the drop-down menus to select a different font and size. Click either checkbox to make the text bold and/or italic.

Next Steps: Export Audio Files

There's never enough rehearsal time for young ensembles. Students can practice their parts on their own, but the nuances of ensemble playing are only learned in context. Notion can quickly and easily export any combination of tracks as .wav files to use as backing tracks. While audio tracks are not a substitute for the live ensemble, they can help students see how they fit in the piece and make rehearsal time more efficient. Of course, this can work for any genre, not just this piece.

Setting the Outputs

Figure 8-14. Export Audio options.

The output options in the Export Audio dialog are Master, Buses, or Instruments. By assigning tracks to buses in the mixer you can export backing tracks for each instrument all at once.

The Mixer

Notion includes a powerful 32-out, 8-bus mixer. We looked at the mixer briefly in Chapter 6. Now, we'll look at some of it in a little more detail.

Choose Window > Show Mixer (⌘ + / [slash] / Ctrl + /) or Click the Mixer button in the Toolbar.

Channel Strips—Instrument

Each instrument is assigned to a channel strip that includes four inserts slots for effects, eight send knobs, solo and mute buttons, true stereo pan controls, and a volume control. The track name is automatically displayed.

Buses

A bus is a path in a mixer where you can route multiple signals. In mixers they are most often used as auxiliary sends for effects. Part of the signal is split from a track and sent to the bus where effects can be applied separately and then added back into the mix. The other main purpose is to create subgroups so that a group of instruments can be mixed using one set of controls.

Eight buses are available in the mixer and each channel has eight corresponding Send knobs. To send part of the signal to a bus, double-click the knob on that track and type in a value. The sends are post-fader, meaning any adjustments you make to the main volume slider on that track will affect the volume of the send as well. On the other hand, the send value will have no effect on the main output signal for the track.

Creating the Submixes

To create the submixes, we'll assign each instrument to three different buses. Use Table 8-4 as a guide and set each send indicated to 100%. So for example, double-click sends A, B, and D on the tenor sax track and type 100%. Normally, a send would not be set to 100%, but in this case we want the submix to be exactly the same as the main mix, only minus one instrument.

	Soprano	Alto	Tenor	Baritone
Bus A		√	√	√
Bus B	√		√	√
Bus C	√	√		√
Bus D	√	√	√	

Table 8-4. Bus assignments.

To check the content and output of any of the buses, click the solo button. You'll hear each has only three instruments.

Exporting the Audio Files

Audio can be exported to disk or directly to your account at SoundCloud (www.soundcloud.com), a free, cloud-based server for sharing and storing audio files. Audio files are in .wav format and can be 16, 24, or 32 bit. Notion will export the file at the same sample rate as the sample set you are using, either 44.1 kHz (CD quality) or 48 kHz (most film and video).

You can export the overall mix or individual buses or individual instruments also known as stems. These stems can then be imported into any DAW for additional processing. For this project we want the output from the buses. To export audio to SoundCloud, you will need to login and enter a code. Skip those steps when exporting to the disk.

- Select File > Export Audio.
- Tick "Upload to SoundCloud."
- Click Connect. Enter your login information, after which you'll be given a code.
- Copy the code (⌘ + C / Ctrl + C) and paste (⌘ + V / Ctrl + V) in the dialog box in Notion.
- Select the bit depth (16 bit is recommended).
- Select Offline.
- Select Buses.
- Click OK.

Notion will export a file for all eight buses, but only the first four will have any audio. You can delete the other four tracks.

Summary

Once again, we covered a lot of new ground, and while there are a lot of steps, you'll be surprised at just how quickly you can produce an arrangement once you get the hang of it. There are literally thousands of Standard MIDI Files of public-domain masterworks that can be used to create arrangements like this for your chamber ensembles.

You should now know how to do the following:

- Import Standard MIDI Files
- Convert Sequencer staves to Notation
- Clear velocities
- Create trills
- Swap voices
- Paste to Voices
- Check ranges
- Add articulations using shortcuts
- Add dynamics using shortcuts
- Add and edit headers and footers
- Format the layout of scores and parts
- Change text fonts
- Add rehearsal letters
- Export audio

Chapter 9

NTEMPO AND LIVE PERFORMANCE

Computers play music perfectly. This might sound like a good idea, but it really ends up sounding mechanical and very unmusical, something for which notation programs are notorious. Notion sounds better than most automatically, but it also includes some unique tools to help your files sound even more expressive and realistic. Better yet, not only can this create a recorded performance, it can also be used in real time.

As we've seen, MusicXML files are used to share files between different notation programs. Because they are print-oriented, they provide much more detail and accuracy than MIDI Files do. The tradeoff is that they provide much less performance data. In the long run, MusicXML files will save time over MIDI files, but will require some editing of performance data to take full advantage of Notion's playback capabilities.

Project Overview

You will import a MusicXML file of a movement from Grieg's *Peer Gynt Suite*. You will edit the file to improve the performance and then use Notion's NTempo feature to conduct the piece and provide realistic tempo adjustments. Finally, you'll mix the performance and export the audio. Numerous files are provided to help you along the way, but as always, I encourage you to use one of your own pieces for this project. You can still follow along with the steps and the results will be of immediate use to you.

New Topics	New Shortcuts	
• Clear tempo • Hide staves • Custom views	. . (period 2 times)	Palette 5: *cresc.*
	, , (comma 2 times)	Palette 5: *dim.*
• Text *cresc.* and *dim.* • Set as Tacet	' (apostrophe)	Express entry
• Tweak dynamics • Randomizing attacks, releases, and velocities	/ / / (slash 3 times)	Palette 6: Unmeasured roll
• Sequencer overlay • NTempo staves	⌘ + ` / Ctrl + `	Switch windows
• Recording tempo maps	F9	Jump to rehearsal letter
• Live Performance mode • Mixing the orchestra	⌘ + G / Ctrl + G	Jump to measure

Table 9-1. New topics and shortcuts.

Basic Procedure

1. Import the file.
2. Clear velocities and tempo information.
3. Edit hairpins and dynamics.
4. Tweak dynamics.
5. Randomize velocities, attacks, and durations.
6. Add other performance techniques.
7. Add an NTempo staff.
8. Record the tempo map.
9. Mix the orchestra.

Step by Step

Importing the File

Use either the Import icon on the Startup Screen or choose File > Import (⌘-Shift + I / Ctrl-Shift + I) and locate the file "MorningMood.xml" (online).

Clear Velocities and Recorded Tempo

We'll clear the recorded velocities (loudness) as most other programs don't handle them as well as Notion does. Dynamics won't be affected, only the velocities of individual notes. Also clear the recorded tempo information, which could interfere with our performance later.

- Type ⌘ + A / Ctrl + A (Edit > Select All).
- Choose Tools > Clear Velocities.
- Choose Tools > Clear Recorded Tempo.

Customizing Your View

Working with large ensemble scores can be unwieldy. You may find it easier if you work in Continuous view (View > Continuous). This view has the music flow from left to right as if on a scroll read horizontally.

Another useful thing to do is to hide staves when you aren't working with them. Choose Score > Score Setup and click the Eye icon for any instrument you want to hide. The staves will still play back, even while hidden.

You should also get in the habit of actively using the Zoom controls, In (⌘ + = / Ctrl + =) and Out (⌘ + - / Ctrl + - [dash]), to create what amounts to screen sets.

Zoom in until an instrument section fills the screen. This has the added advantage of making it easy to move to other sections, unlike hidden staves. If there are more or fewer instruments in the section, just zoom in or out as necessary.

Measure Numbers

It will also help to have measure numbers on every measure while we are working. You can change them back later if you like.

- Choose Score > Full Score Options.
- Click the Layout tab.
- Set Measure numbers to "Each measure."

▶ Open the file "MorningMood-edit.notion" to begin here.

Crescendos, Decrescendos, and Diminuendos

Notation programs vary in how they handle gradual dynamic changes, and this doesn't necessarily translate from one program to the next in MusicXML files. As discussed in Chapter 8, in order to play back correctly, the beginning and end of the hairpin must be attached to a note with the dynamic marking. So, you need to check whether they are playing back correctly on imported files. Locate a crescendo that should be clearly audible in one instrument. Select the measures involved and press Play (spacebar). If you don't hear an audible difference, you will need to re-enter the hairpins and text *cresc.* and *dim.* expressions.

The example file was saved using Notion (after being imported from another program), so most of the dynamics will play back correctly. However, there are a few places where we will need to make some adjustments.

The Crescendo/Decrescendo Pair

One of the more common indications in this score is the crescendo followed immediately by a decrescendo with no dynamic levels indicated. Human players have no problem understanding this, but not so with computers. A dynamic needs to be placed at the end of the crescendo and again at the end of the decrescendo.

> ❶ **TIP:** A special case is when you want to have the volume decrease to nothing. In that case, enter a decrescendo and attach the end to a barline.

In the last three measures, just such a crescendo/decrescendo pair occurs in all instruments.

Figure 9-1. The crescendo/decrescendo pair.

Select these measures (click-drag-enclose or double-click/Shift-click) for one of the instruments and listen to the playback. The dynamic change will be very subtle if there's any effect at all. There should be a big swell and fade there, so we will need to add dynamics.

- Type ff (Palette 4: *ff*), then click under the second of the three notes in clarinet 2 (you'll see why shortly).

- Delete both hairpins.
- Type , [comma] and click below the first note, then click the second note.
- Type . [period] and click below the second note, then click the final barline.

If this score were to be used for parts, we would then hide the dynamics. But for this example, think of it as a conductor's score where markings such as these would be penciled in anyway. If parts that conform to the original score are needed, simply duplicate the score before editing.

That took quite a few steps, and doing that for each instrument would be quite time consuming. But there's a workaround available. All of the instruments are playing the same rhythm. We can copy and paste these three measures and then change the notes using the arrow keys much more quickly than entering the dynamics. We chose the second clarinet part as it was in the middle of the staff and wouldn't end up in an extreme range when copied to other instruments.

- Select the three measures of the clarinet 2 part.
- Type ⌘ + C / Ctrl + C (Edit > Copy).
- Double-click the first of the corresponding measures (m. 85) in the flute 1 bar. Pay attention to the note in that measure (high E).
- Type ⌘ + V / Ctrl + V (Edit > Paste); the pasted measure will be selected.
- While the pasted section is still selected, type ⌘-Shift + ↑ / Ctrl-Shift + ↑ [up arrow key] twice to transpose up two octaves.
- Type ↓ [down arrow key] twice to move down two steps.

Now repeat this step for all instruments with one note, being sure to observe the note that is being replaced. Save divisi instruments for last, and either manually enter the dynamics or manually add the second note and ties. Both will take about the same time, so it's your call.

Text Crescendo and Diminuendo

The text expressions *cresc.* and *dim.* both behave in the same way as the hairpins and need to be attached to notes with dynamics or a barline so as to play back correctly. Look at the section from measures 36–40 in the strings. Select the strings for those measures and press Play to hear how they sound.

- Select and delete the existing *cresc. molto* and *dim.* in violins 1 and 2, viola, and cello.
- Type , , (comma, two times) (Palette 5: *cresc . . .*).
- Click Violin 1, m. 36, beat 2, then click the downbeat of m. 38.
- Repeat for violin 2 and viola.
- Click Cello m. 36, beat 1, then click the downbeat of m. 38.
- Type . . (period, two times) (Palette 5: *dim . . .*).
- Click Violin 1, m. 38, beat 2, then click the downbeat of m. 40.
- Repeat for violin 2 and viola.

Now select the strings for the section and press Play. You'll hear a big difference.

● Open "MorningMood-overlay.notion" to begin here.

Unsupported Dynamics

Notion handles the playback for dynamics located Palette 5, but it does not support playback for those in Palette 4, nor those entered manually or with Express Entry. There is a workaround if it's important.

In measures 81–83, *forte-pianos* (*fp*) are indicated in oboe 1 and the clarinets. To make the playback correct, you will need to create a new staff with the same instrument and enter the notes as dynamics as follows. Then hide the new staves and set the written staves to Tacet for those measures.

Figure 9-2. The *forte-piano* (*fp*) as written.

Figure 9-3. The *fp* in playback.

- Type ⌘ + T / Ctrl + T (Score > Score Setup).
- Add two clarinets and one oboe.
- Drag the staves so they are each below the written instrument.
- Click the Track Setup icon for sounding clarinet 1.
- Select Notation and set the transposition to A.
- Repeat for the sounding clarinet 2.
- Exit Score Setup.
- Enter the notes and dynamics as shown in Figure 9-3 in the sounding clarinet 1 part.
- Select, copy, and paste the three measures to sounding clarinet 2.
- Transpose down a third (press the down arrow twice).
- Paste to the oboe 1 part.
- Re-pitch or drag the notes to the correct pitches.
- Delete the tie between mm. 81 and 82.

To complete the process, hide the sounding instruments and set the notes in the written instruments to Tacet.

- Type ⌘ + T / Ctrl + T (Score > Score Setup).
- Click the Eye icon for the three sounding instruments, to hide them.
- Press Esc.
- Select mm. 81–83 in oboe 1 and clarinets 1 and 2.
- Right-click and choose Notes > Set as Tacet.

This is a lot of work for a large score, so be sure it's necessary.

Tweaking Dynamics

From letter A to B, there is a very gradual crescendo from *forte* to *fortissimo* indicated by some hairpins without dynamics followed by *più f* (more *forte*) three measures before letter B. We can get this effect by tweaking the dynamics.

- Mac: triple-click Flute 1, m. 27.
- Windows: double-click Flute 1, Shift-click Double Bass.
- Right-click and choose Tools > Tweak Dynamics.
- Enter 0.49 (any value 0.5 and above changes the dynamic to the next value).
- Press Return/Enter.

To make this even more effective, enter a *forte* (F) after the crescendo in measure 23 and tweak it up by 0.2. Then tweak the dynamic in measure 21 down slightly by –0.2.

Randomizing Attacks and Velocities

Beginning at letter A, there are a lot of very large chords in the winds. Of course, the computer attacks them perfectly on the beat, with the result being a very unnatural, organlike sound. We can quickly make this sound more realistic by randomizing very slightly. Good musicians never really play randomly, but they do interpret differently. One player might be consistently ahead of the beat slightly, while another is behind. Applying randomization like this works because we are applying it to a large group of instruments. Each instrument soloed will not sound correct as it will move from before, on, and after the beat randomly, but together it works.

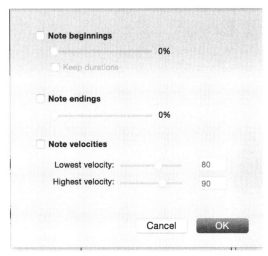

Figure 9-4. Randomize options.

- Select mm. 21–24 for all instruments from flute 1 to horns 3–4.
- Choose Tools > Randomize Events.
- Check Note Beginnings and set to 2%.
- Check Note Endings and set to 1%.

Play the section. The effect is subtle, but that doesn't make it any less important. Use your ear rather your eyes. Randomize a little more, if so desired.

> **TIP:** For an even better realization, use ⌘-click / Ctrl-click to choose only one instrument from each section. This ensures that one instrument in each section will be right on the beat and at the velocity specified by the score.

Other Performance-Based Edits

The timpani rolls did not make it through the MusicXML process, so we'll need to add them manually.

- Type / / / (slash, three times) (Palette 6: Unmeasured Roll).
- Click on the timpani notes in m. 20, mm. 56–61, and mm. 85 and 86.

Using the Sequencer Overlay

The Sequencer Overlay lets us adjust the length and velocity of individual notes without changing the notation. Press the Tab key to display it. Zoom in (⌘ + = / Ctrl + =) for more precise control.

- **To change the length of a note:** Click the right end of the horizontal bar and drag left or right.
- **To change the start time of a note:** Click the left end of the horizontal bar and drag left or right.

Figure 9-5. Overlapping release and attacks.

Adjusting every single note in this manner is probably not worth the effort, but you'll find that by only changing solos or the lead voice of the section you can dramatically improve the phrasing. For slurred notes, move the release of each note to overlap the start of the next note slightly. In most cases, Notion will play a sample that isn't attacked as hard as normal notes, but if they are detached at all, the effect will be minimal.

▶ Open "MorningMood-perform.notion" to begin here.

NTempo

Recording and controlling tempos in real time is done using an NTempo staff. The NTempo staff only appears on the screen; it doesn't print or play. Notes are placed in the staff and you tap the computer keyboard or a MIDI key to control the tempo.

To Create an NTempo Staff
- Open Score Setup.
- Choose Special > NTempo.

There are quite a few options for what you place in an NTempo staff. The simplest option is to place one note per beat. However, that won't always result in the best playback. Another option is to copy the most prominent line from your score. This might produce too many impulses and make the music less smooth. My preference is to use as few impulses as possible, generally following the pulse rather than the beat. Ideally, set it up as you would conduct or perform it.

You can place notes into the NTempo staff and duplicate when the meter is the same throughout, but for something with changing meters, the simplest option will be to step-time record.
- Double-click the first measure of the NTempo staff.
- Click the Step-time Record button.
- Enter notes on B4 (B above middle C) using the shortcuts W, H, Q, and E.

Live Performance Mode

Tapping a key on your MIDI or computer keyboard controls the tempo. The MIDI keyboard will be more responsive than the computer keyboard and has some additional navigation functions, so I recommend you use it when available.

Set Up the MIDI Keyboard for NTempo
- Choose Notion > Preferences / File > Preferences.
- Select the MIDI tab.
- Set NTempo channel to 1 (or any channel that your MIDI keyboard supports).

To perform the score live, click the Live Performance Mode button. Then begin tapping the rhythm of the notes in the NTempo staff on your computer or MIDI keyboard. Notion will play each beat at the exact time you tap. It will take a little practice if you put in anything more complex than the beats. We'll explore some more of the additional commands for live performance mode later in this chapter.

Recording the Tempo Map

Recording the tempo map is the same as Live Performance Mode except you record the tempo. Click the Tempo Overdub button and tap a computer or MIDI key to perform the score as you did in Live Performance. You can stop at any time and start recording again if you make a major mistake. Just press Esc, click the note where you want to start, and continue tapping.

Editing the Tempo Map

Even though you can overdub the NTempo track, it will still take a little practice to get the tempo just right. You may be mostly satisfied with the tempo map, but need to adjust one or two beats here and there. The recorded tempo markers give a visual clue to what was recorded. You can quickly see if the tempo is faster or slower than the tempo of the piece and by approximately how much. In this way you can quickly spot outliers.

To Edit the Tempo Marker

- Click on the marker. It will display the percentage of the original tempo at that point.
- Drag up or down to change the tempo.

Figure 9-6. Recorded tempo markers.

Mixing the Orchestra

With all the notes, dynamics, articulations, and other edits completed, when working with virtual orchestras, your job is only half finished. Blend is primarily achieved through good orchestration practices, but you still have to pull it all together in the final mixdown.

The Mixer

Most of the time, I prefer to let the mixer float, allowing the window I'm working on to move to the top, and use the shortcut ⌘ + ` / Ctrl + ` to switch windows. If you have two monitors, place the mixer on one and the notation on the other. If you have only a single monitor, for this section you'll probably want to keep the mixer visible. Open the Preferences window and under the General tab, select "Keep Mixer on Top."

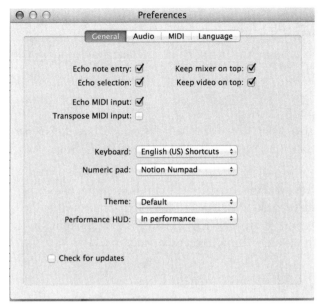

Figure 9-7. The General Preferences tab.

The mixer will handle all of the tracks of the orchestra, but 17 tracks are a little unwieldy. We can use some of the mixer's features to make them a little more manageable. The buttons on the left side let you quickly choose a group of tracks to display. You can choose instrument channels, the eight bus tracks, or any of the groups Notion automatically creates based on instrument families for built-in instruments and for external VSTis and ReWire.

Figure 9-8. Mixer track groups.

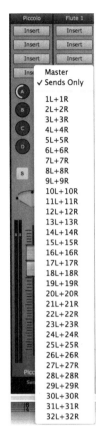

Figure 9-9. Channel outputs.

Setting the Output

The current output is displayed at the bottom of the channel strip. Click on it to display the available outputs. For this example, set all of the channel outputs to "Sends Only."

Creating the Subgroups

We first looked at creating submixes in the last chapter. For this orchestra, assign each instrument section to a separate subgroup, which will make mixing much easier.

To assign a track to a subgroup, double-click on the knob corresponding to the group (see Table 9-2) and type the value. For now, set each send to 75%.

Instrument	Bus	Instrument	Bus
Flutes	A	Horns	E
Oboes	B	Trumpets	F
Clarinets	C	Timpani	G
Bassoons	D	Strings	H

Table 9-2. Subgroup assignments.

Balancing Each Section

As Notion is using the same set of samples for each like instrument, the balance should already be pretty good. But you may want to adjust it slightly to tune the chords a little better or bring out the lead line. Remember, all of the sends in the mixer are post-fader. Any adjustments to the channel volume fader will affect the level sent to the bus, too.

Work section by section first. Click the Woodwinds button and click the solo button for the flutes. Adjust the balance between the two flutes. You may want to begin adjusting the EQ as well, applying it to compensate for any perceived weakness in the samples. Repeat with each section until you are satisfied with the balance of each individual section.

Articulations

As you go through this process, you may notice that you don't like the sounds of some of the written articulations. You can experiment with different articulations or none at all.

Panning the Individual Instruments

The overall panning will be done on the bus tracks, so at this stage just spread the instruments across the field. In this MusicXML file, all of the instruments are panned dead center. As this is a true stereo pan control, there are three control points, but they are all at the center. The left and right points control the stereo spread of the sound and the perceived distance from the microphone; a narrower field will sound closer. Take care to not cross the left and right pan points as this will put the samples out of phase. Out-of-phase panning will be displayed in pink, in-phase in gray. With two instruments in the section, set one to center-left and one to center-right. The width should be slightly more than half of the field, with some overlap with the lead instrument in the center.

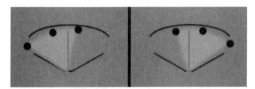

Figure 9-10. Panning for sections with two instruments.

Panning Strings

There is no one correct way to pan strings. Some set them as they are found in the orchestra, from left to right violins 1, violins 2, violas, cellos, and basses, which produces a more natural sound but often lacks bottom. Others suggest setting the cellos and basses in the center, violins 1 on the left, violins 2 on the right, and the violas between the second violins and the cellos. This gives more weight to the mix as the basses and cellos stand out, but others hear it as unnatural. It really comes down to a matter of taste. For now, use the second option as shown in Figure 9-11. Orchestras are not close-miked, so set the spread to around 40 percent of the stereo field with plenty of overlap.

Figure 9-11. Strings panning positions.

Balancing the Orchestra

With each section individually balanced, it's time to put it all together to create the full ensemble. We only need to see the buses and the master, so make sure both are selected. Because there are only built-in instruments here, click the ReWire or VSTi button to hide all the instrument channels.

Adjusting the Pan Setting

The rest of the orchestra is usually panned to somewhat match the physical layout of the ensemble. The strings' panning has already been set, so its bus should be panned center and use the entire stereo field. Flutes, clarinets, and horns will be left center; oboes, bassoons, and brass will be right center. The timpani should be set in the center. Try to give each instrument its own spot, but don't pan anything all the way right or left. Experiment with the width of the stereo field, but somewhere around 25 to 33 percent should work. Tightening the field places the instruments closer to the microphone, so don't be tempted to make the field too narrow. You can also set the back-row instruments a little wider than second- and third-row players.

Figure 9-12. Bus panning.

EQ

Now is a good time to look at EQ, which we first looked at in Chapter 6. Listen to the overall sound. For sections, use it to help fit the pieces together tighter without increasing the overall volume. Add an EQ to each bus channel. Listen to the overall sound of the ensemble. Sometimes, a soloed section can sound great, but when added to the mix, it sounds like bunch of soloists. Your goal is to blend the ensemble together to create a unified sound. Avoid the temptation to boost too much. Often, if one section is not being heard, a cut in the section covering it up or even just the a cut in one frequency range is the answer.

Section Reverb

Reverb is most often used on the master to simulate a room space. But if your computer is powerful enough, you can apply the reverb to each bus separately. The advantage of this is that you can set different pre-delay times for the sections, which will give a more three-dimensional aspect to the mix.

Set the pre-delay for the strings at about 40–50 ms and then increase it by 5–10 ms for each row in the seating chart (see Table 9-3), flutes and oboes, clarinets and bassoons, horns, brass, and percussion. It's a subtle effect and you'll need to use your ears. One trick is to increase it until it's noticeable and then back it off some. Don't spread things out too much, as the goal is still to have a uniform ensemble.

Instrument	Pre-delay Time
Strings	45 ms
Flutes/oboes	52 ms
Clarinets/bassoons	59 ms
Horns	67 ms
Brass	74 ms
Percussion	80 ms

Table 9-3. Pre-delay times.

Another trick is to sync the pre-delay times to the tempo. Set the front section to a sixty-fourth-note and the back section to a thirty-second and then balance the other sections in between. This can result in a slightly tighter sound. To get the values, divide 60,000 by the tempo to get the quarter-note and then divide by 16 for the sixty-fourth-note and by 8 for the thirty-second. For example, at 120 M.M., 60,000/90 = 667 ms per quarter-note; 667/16 = 42 ms and 667/8 = 84 ms. In a piece such as this, it will be less important, as most notes are quarters or eighths.

Mastering

Mastering is a completely separate art form. Notion's tools for mastering are limited and for a really good master, you should either export to your DAW or use third-party VST plug-ins. But for now, we'll use Notion's built-in effects.

Reverb

Place this in the first insert. For a big hall sound, increase the pre-delay to about 40–50 ms, which will give the effect of sitting in the middle of the hall, and start with the wet/dry mix at 50%. If you find that to be a little bit too much, reduce the wet/dry mix until you are satisfied. The room should be large, so leave it at around 90%.

Master EQ

Place this in the second insert. The EQ to the Master bus is used as a mastering EQ to apply the finishing touches to make the mix really sing. For this you really need to use your ear. It's also a good idea to not use headphones if at all possible. Generally speaking, at this point all adjustments should be pretty subtle, so start with ±1.0 dB. The bandwidth Q should be fairly wide; the default 0.6 should be fine. Clear any soloed sections and insert an EQ onto the Master channel. There are no hard-and-fast rules here, but some general guidelines follow. Experiment until it sounds good to your ear.

- If the mix is too bright or dull, adjust the HF (high frequency) or MHF (mid-high frequency).
- If the mix is muddy, reduce the MHF and MLF (mid-low frequency).
- If it is boomy or doesn't have enough gravitas, adjust the LF (low frequency) and MLF.

A full tutorial on EQ is beyond the scope of this book, but a great interactive guide can be found at http://www.independentrecording.net/irn/resources/freqchart/main_display.htm.

Limiter

The last item in the chain is a limiter. You don't want your mix to bump into this at all, but it's still a good idea to have it, as one spike can ruin a good recording. Set it to –0.1 dB to prevent any chance of clipping.

Next Steps: Ensemble Accompanist

The possibilities for NTempo and Live Performance modes are endless. Notion is already being used in Broadway shows alongside live ensembles. It will make a great rehearsal ensemble for musicals, too. For amateur and semi-professional companies, where the orchestra only comes in the last week or so, this can make a real difference for the cast. In Chapter 11 we'll look at some advanced controls that will make it an even better rehearsal accompanist.

In education, consider using Notion in conducting classes, as is done at the Berklee College of Music. No more conducting to static recordings. With three or four (or more) computers running Notion, each with a different section of the ensemble, aspiring conductors can get a feel for how an orchestra responds to their directions without leaving the classroom.

One real possibility is for use as a choral accompanist. In these days of budget cuts, it's often hard to have an accompanist day in and day out, particularly at the elementary level. This leaves choral teachers with the unenviable task of trying to conduct the ensemble from behind an upright piano while playing the accompaniment. With Notion you can tap a single key on the computer or MIDI keyboard, allowing you to conduct with the other hand. The Max patcher included online will let you tap a sustain pedal attached to a MIDI keyboard to control NTempo, freeing you to conduct with both hands. You will need to download the free Max Runtime application from the Cycling 74 website (http://cycling74.com/downloads/runtime/). Then open the file "Sustain2C4.maxpat" on the website, open Notion's Preferences, and set the NTempo channel to 16 and MIDI input devices to All.

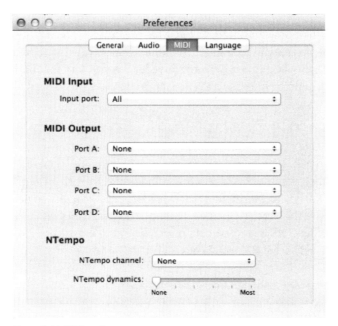

Figure 9-13. MIDI preferences.

For any live performance situation, navigating is easy. Use the Navigate button in the Toolbar (F9) to quickly jump to any rehearsal letters. You can also jump to any measure by typing ⌘ + G / Ctrl + G and entering the measure number or rehearsal letter.

Summary

This chapter was all about playback, which is one of the main features that sets Notion apart from other notation programs. Live Performance mode offers a wealth of possibilities for the professional, amateur, or educator. Recording a tempo map makes a static computer performance come to life. The controls available for dynamics and articulation also help create a more realistic performance. Tweaking the MIDI note data takes that a step further.

Here are the things you should know how to do after completing this chapter.

- Clear tempo and velocity data
- Hide staves
- Hide Attachments
- Edit hairpins for playback
- Enter text dynamic changes
- Tweak dynamics levels
- Effectively randomize attacks and velocities
- Create NTempo staves
- Conduct a score in real time
- Record tempo map
- Mix the orchestra

Chapter 10
SOLO PIANO

Solo piano music presents the most challenging problems for a notation program. Multiple voices per staff, cross-staff beaming, grace notes, clef changes, and extensive phrasing and articulations combine to make it difficult, even for the experienced copyist.

Project Overview

In this project, we'll enter an excerpt from a Chopin *Valse* that includes all of the above notation features. The example looks longer than it is. Look closely and you'll see that quite a few sections are repeated. The tendency for most people is to jump right in and start entering notes. This example will show you how a little planning beforehand will save a lot of time. Using Copy and Paste is by far the fastest way to enter music.

The completed score for this example can be found as a PDF file online. Open the file "Chopin_Valse.pdf" to proceed with the project. The original published score on which this example is based was downloaded from IMSLP, the Petrucci Music Library of public-domain works (http://www.imslp.org).

New Topics	New Shortcuts	
• Pedals • Edit beaming • Cross-staff beams • Grace notes • Clef changes	Shift + B	Palette 3: Beam tool
	8, 88	Palette 6: Ped, *
	Shift + A	Palette 6: Arpeggio
	GGG	Palette 3: 16th-note grace note
	C	Palette 9: Treble Clef
	CCC	Palette 9: Bass Clef
	Shift + 8	Palette 9: 8va
	Shift + - (dash)	Palette 8: Tempo
	R	Palette 8: Ritard
	RR	Palette 8: Accelerando

Table 10-1. New topics and shortcuts.

Basic Procedure

1. Analyze the form.
2. Set up the score—meter, key, pickup measure.
3. Enter notes for the first two phrases.
4. Edit the sections.
5. Copy and paste to complete the section.
6. Enter notes for the third and fourth phrases.
7. Copy and paste to complete the section.
8. Add repeats and endings.
9. Adjust the layout.
10. Enter hidden tempo changes to improve playback.

Step by Step

Planning

Form

The excerpt has two sections with 56 measures, but upon closer examination we see that there are actually only four distinct 8-measure phrases. We will only enter each once and then use Copy and Paste to create the form.

A	‖: B :‖	C	D	‖: B :‖
8 measures	8 measures	8 measures	8 measures	8 measures

Table 10-2. Phrase structure.

Note Entry

Although it's possible to enter this in real time, it's probably going to be more efficient to use step-time recording with or without a MIDI keyboard. The challenge in real time would be to not play the grace notes and to play the measures with two voices clearly enough so Notion would get it close. The unison notes are unlikely to be interpreted correctly, in any case. You also need to go back and enter articulations separately. In step-time recording, you will enter the notes and the articulations together and there will be fewer errors. But the choice is yours.

Now, look through the piece to identify the areas that deserve extra thought. Most of the piece can be entered in voice 1. However, the first two measures present a challenge; the second measure has cross-staff notes. We will need to decide whether to enter them in the treble or bass staff before applying the cross-staff function. Because there is a slur over the first three measures, all three measures will need to be in the same voice and staff. In most cases, you will need to experiment to see which works best. As it turns out, entering the first three measures of eighth-notes in voice 1 in the treble staff will produce the best results.

There are notes that will go into voice 2 in the second phrase along with some grace notes. Grace notes can only be entered in Edit mode, so that's probably the best way to enter the voice 2 notes as well. But notice there are two voices only on beats 2 and 3. In voice 1, we will enter a rest on beat 1, followed by the half-note, and then hide the rest.

All other entries will be added in Edit mode. We'll also have to fix some enharmonic spelling, change some stem directions, set the cross-staff notes, and make some beam adjustments.

Score Setup

Create a New Score
- From the startup screen, select New Score or type ⌘ + N / Ctrl + N (File > New).
- From the instrument palettes, select Keyboards/Harp > Piano.
- Click Exit Score setup or press Esc.

Set the Meter and Key
The piece is in E minor and the meter is 3/4.
- Type Shift + K.
- Set Tonic to E and Mode to Minor.
- Press Return/Enter.
- Click in the first measure.
- Type Shift + M.
- Set Upper to 3 and Lower to 4.
- Press Return/Enter.

Create the Pickup Measure
- Right-click m. 1.
- Choose Measure 1 > Pickup Measure.
  Note: The pickup measure will be counted as measure 0.

Note Entry: Sections A and B

▶ If you would prefer to skip note entry, open the file "Valse-notes.notion" (online) and copy and paste the notes as needed.

Real-Time Recording
If you have the piano skills, you might be tempted to try to record this into both staves at once. Before you do, you will need to identify the split point, the note above which notes go in the right hand and below in the left hand. The split point is fixed in Notion, but you can always stop, change it, and continue. To identify the split point, locate the lowest note in the right hand and the highest in the left hand. The split point needs to be between those two notes.

However, in this piece, the ranges of the left and right hands overlap too often for two-staff recording to be an option. Therefore, record the right hand followed by the left hand. Set the tempo to something comfortable. Do not play expressively. Focus on accuracy for notation purposes, not performance. Play the notes marked 8va at the written pitch, not an octave higher. As noted above, the measures with voice 2 will not be interpreted correctly, so play only one voice in those measures.

- Type ⌘ + R / Ctrl + R or click the Record button.
- Set the minimum duration to (30,000/tempo) ms, but not more than an eighth-note.
- Set the split point to C3 (an octave below middle C).
- Un-tick Tuplets and Multi-voice.
- Press the spacebar and record the right-hand part through m. 16, including the eighth-notes in the first two measures.

You can stop anywhere along the way and restart, but first delete any notes that are to be replaced. When the right hand is completed, record the left-hand part, changing the split point to C5.

Step-time Recording

As the notated rhythm is not very complex, step-time recording will be almost as fast, if not faster, than real-time entry. As in real-time recording, play the notes at the written pitch, ignoring the 8va indications for now. Enter only voice 1 and add the articulations as you go. Enter the right hand first, followed by the left hand.

Editing Sections A and B

Because section B will be copied and pasted a number of times, all the other entries and editing should be completed first. Press Esc to enter Edit mode. Zoom in (⌘ + = / Ctrl + =) a bit to make the mouse work a little easier. The following list is a suggestion. You can do these in just about any order, though I do recommend saving the slurs for last. It looks like a lot of steps, but you'll be surprised at how quick and easy it really is.

Check for Errors

Look over the entries and make sure the notes and rhythms are correct. A couple of notes likely will need to be respelled enharmonically (Shift + E). Make sure all articulations have been entered as well.

To change the pitch of a note: Click the notehead and use the up and down arrow keys.

To change the rhythmic value of a note: Click the notehead and type = [equal sign] followed by the shortcut for the correct note value.

Enter Articulations (If Needed)
- Type 1 (Palette 4: Staccato).
- Click on the notes.

Enter Grace Notes
- Type GGG for sixteenth-note grace notes.
- Point and click to enter sixteenth-note grace notes in mm. 11, 13, 14, and 15.

Adjust Beaming

The eighth-notes should all be beamed together in each measure. Stem direction will change automatically to create the beams when necessary.

Figure 10-1. Beam selected.

- Type Shift + B.
- Click between notes where beams are needed.
- Press Esc.

A special case is the beam over the sixteenth-rest in measure 7. Click on the eighth-note before the rest to beam. Then click on the beam and adjust it to clear the rest.

Enter Voice 2

The notes in voice 2 in measures 13–15 can be entered in a nonlinear way. After all the notes are entered, hide the rests.

- Type ⌘ + 2 / Ctrl + 2.
- Type QQ.
- Click in mm. 13, 14, and 15.
- Type E.
- Enter the eighth-notes in mm. 13–15.
- Type Q.
- Enter the quarter-notes in mm. 13–15.
- Select (click/Shift-click) the rests in mm. 13–15.
- Right-click and choose Rests > Hide Rests.

Enter the Clef Changes

There are a couple of clef changes in the left hand.

- Type C (Palette 9: Treble Clef).
- Click between beats 1 and 2, m. 14.
- Type CCC (Palette 9: Bass Clef).
- Click before beat 1, m. 15.
- Type C (Palette 9: Treble Clef).
- Click between beats 1 and 2, m. 15.
- Type CCC (Palette 9: Bass Clef).
- Click in m. 17.

Flip Stem Direction

The stems in measure 4 should be down.

- Double-click m. 4.
- Right-click and choose Notes > Stems Down.

Slurs

Slurs need to be entered before cross-staff notes are moved.

- Make sure you are in voice 1.
- Type Shift + S.
- Click the first note of m. 1.
- Click the last note of m. 3.
- Continue until all slurs have been entered.

Slurs can be placed above or below the staff. The placement of slurs varies from edition to edition, and we'll use the placement that gives the best appearance.

- Click the slur between the grace notes and first note of m. 16.
- Right-click and choose Attachments > Show Below Staff.
- Repeat with the slurs in the bass clef of mm. 14 and 15.

To delete a slur, select it and press Delete/Backspace.

Dynamics

Remember to enter the dynamics before the entering crescendos.

- Type P (Palette 4: *p*).
- Click in mm. 0 and 9.
- Type F (Palette 4: *f*).
- Click in m. 7.
- Type , , [2 commas] (Palette 4: <).
- Click below beat 3, m. 3.
- Click the *f* in m. 7.

The Octave Setting (8va)

- Type Shift + 8 (Palette 9: 8va).
- Click the last note in m. 7.
- Click the first note in m. 8.
- Click the first grace note in m. 11.
- Click the last note of m. 16.

Other Entries

The remaining entries, pedal markings (ped) and arpeggios, can be entered together or separately.

- Type 8 (Palette 6: Ped).
- Click below m. 3.
- Type 8 8 (Palette 6: * [asterisk]).
- Click below m. 4.
- Type Shift + A (Palette 6: Arpeggio).
- Click the chords in mm. 3–7.
- Continue entering pedal on and off markings.

Set the Cross-staff Notes

All of the notes in from the pickup measure through the third note in measure 2 need to be placed in the bass clef staff. The beams will need to be adjusted after the notes are moved.

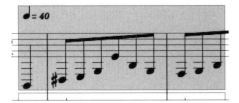

Figure 10-2. Notes selected for cross-staff.

- Select (click-drag-enclose) the notes as shown in Figure 10-2.
- Right-click and choose Notes > Cross-staff.
- Click the beam in m. 1 and drag up. Click and drag the end to create a flat beam.
- Click the beam in m. 2 and drag down. Adjust the end to create a flat beam.

Copy and Paste Section B

The B section is repeated exactly, except for the last measure, which we will edit manually. The clef changes will not be copied, so they will need to be entered again.

If you are using the "Valse-Notes" file from the online media, first create a new piano score and copy and paste the completed section A and then copy and paste section B twice.

- Double-click the treble clef staff in m. 9.
- Shift-click the bass clef staff in m. 16.
- Type ⌘ + D / Ctrl + D (Edit > Duplicate).
- Select (click-drag-enclose) the last five eighth-notes in m. 24.
- Press Delete/Backspace.
- Double-click m. 24.
- Type = + Q to change it to a quarter-note.
- Enter the treble clef (C) and bass clef (CCC) changes in mm. 22, 23, and 25.

Note Entry: Sections C and D

We need to add measures before entering the notes for the next two sections. Type I and click repeatedly in the last measure until there are 57 measures. Enter the notes as you did in the first two sections. Note that there is a voice 2 note in measure 39.

Don't forget the articulations, if you are using step-time recording.

Editing Sections C and D

Most of the editing in these sections is the same, but there are a few new ones.

Enharmonics

Notion guessed wrong on the B♭s and entered them as A♯s. The enharmonic tool is only available by using the shortcut.

- Type Shift + E.
- Click on each A♯ in mm. 27 and 35.
- Click on the D♯ in m. 40.
  Complete the remaining edits.
- Enter the note in voice 2 (⌘ + 2 / Ctrl + 2) in m. 39. Hide the rest on beat 1.
- Enter articulations—staccato (1) and accent (5)—if necessary.
- Connect beams (Shift + B).
- Select mm. 36–38 and flip stems down.
- Add pedal markings (8, 88).
- Add slurs (Shift + S).
- Add 8va (Shift + 8).

There's a decrescendo at the end of the last phrase with no dynamics. Enter a *p* on the last note before entering the hairpin. Then right-click and hide the dynamic.

Copy Section B

To complete this section, we'll copy the B sections and then manually edit the last two measures. If you are using the "Valse-Notes file," copy and paste sections C and D first.

- Select (double-click/Shift-click) mm. 9–24.
- Type ⌘ + C / Ctrl + C (Edit > Copy).
- Double-click m. 41.
- Type ⌘ + V / Ctrl + V (Edit > Paste).
- Enter the treble clef (C) and bass clef (CCC) changes in mm. 54 and 55.

Repeats and Endings

- Duplicate m. 56 (⌘ + D / Ctrl + D).
- Delete the last two eighth-notes.
- Add a backward repeat in m. 56 (Shift + ;).
- Add first and second endings in m. 56 (Shift + ; ; ;).
- Add a forward repeat in m. 25 (Shift + ; ;).

Layout

The basic score layout looks pretty good as is, though the number of measures in each system is a little unbalanced and the form is obscured a little. With just a little work, it should look fine.

Right-click measure 25 and choose Measure 25 > Force New System. From here use the same command on various measures to create a balanced look. You should end up with two pages, with five systems on page 1 and six on page 2, each with between four and six measures.

Final Touches

- Double-click the title and type "Valse."
- Double-click Composer and type "Frederic Chopin."
- Double-click Date and type "Posthumous."
- Choose Score > Full Score Options.
- Select the Layout tab.
- Set Titles following to "None."

Playback

The tempo in Chopin piano works is very fluid. This might be a good candidate for NTempo, but we can accomplish much the same just using tempo marks, ritards, and accelerandos. The tempos used here are based on a recording by the great pianist Arthur Rubinstein. Entering these will skew the layout, so hide each one after entering it.

- Double-click the initial tempo mark and type "h=90."
- Type Shift + - [dash] (Palette 9: M.M.).
- Set Tempos as shown in Table 10-3.

Measure	Tempo	Measure	Tempo
9	h=78	39	h=84
24	h=52	40	h=56
25	h=68	41	h=78
33	h=78	57	q=90

Table 10-3. Tempo changes.

Now, a couple of ritards and accelerandos to smooth things out a bit.

- Enter a ritard (R) in m. 23.
- Double-click the ritard and set the destination tempo to 52 bpm.
- Enter an accelerando (RR) in m. 33 and set the destination tempo to 84 bpm.
- Enter a ritard in m. 39 and set the target tempo to 67 bpm.
- Select each tempo marking, then right-click (near, not on) and choose Attachments > Hide.

> **❶ TIP:** You can change the name of the ritard to rall. or whatever you like (faster, slower) at the same time you set the target tempo.

Next Steps: More Notation Challenges

Of course, piano isn't the only instrument with unique notation practices. Let's look at some other common notation issues.

Specific Instrument Techniques

The last palette is one that offers performance techniques that are specific to the selected instrument. To get a feel for what is available, create a score using the full orchestra template. Click on the last palette and then click on each instrument track. All of these techniques will affect playback.

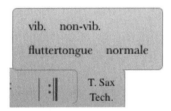

Figure 10-3. Instrument specific techniques palette.

Percussion

Notion has a large collection of pitched and non-pitched percussion instruments. The pitched percussion instruments use standard staves and notation. Non-pitched percussion instruments generally use a single staff line. The various noteheads will trigger different samples on some instruments, as will certain articulations, but may have no effect on others. Many of the percussion instruments have two samples, one triggered by notes above the single line and the other by notes on or below the line. There is also a collection of sound effects samples that can be assigned to percussionists or to their own staff.

Agogô	Log Drum	
Anvil	Maracas	
Bell Tree	Ocean Drum	
Brake Drum	Rainstick	**Strings**
Cabasa	Ratchet	**Woodwinds**
Castanets	Sand Blocks	**Saxophones**
Caxixi	Sleigh Bells	**Brass**
Claves	Slide Whistle	**Guitars/Basses**
Cowbell	Tam-tam	**Keyboards/Harp**
Cuíca	Tambourine	**Drums/Cymbals**
Drum Sticks	Triangle	**Pitched Percussion**
Flexatone	Vibrastick	**Other Percussion**
Ganza	Vibraslap	**Sound Effects**
Gong	Water Gong	**Vocal**
Guiro	Wood Block	**Special**

Figure 10-4. Available percussion instruments.

Harp

Harp tunings are indicated using note names rather than pedals. The cross-staff feature also works for harp and can be useful for glissandos. Be sure to add the glissando by clicking on the first and last note before setting the cross-staff note.

Figure 10-5. Harp techniques.

Microtones

Contemporary composers will be pleased to find that Notion includes a full complement of microtonal accidentals that play back. These include lowered and raised flats, sharps, and naturals. The available accidentals from low to high are shown in Figure 10-6. In general, a raised flat and a lowered natural will have the same tuning, but as different samples are sometimes triggered, you can at times get different effects by using accidentals that should essentially be the same.

Figure 10-6. Accidentals.

Each uses the same shortcut as the standard accidental with the Shift key added. For example, 2 is the shortcut for flat, whereas Shift + 2 is the shortcut for the raised and lowered flats.

Summary

Piano music presents more challenges in standard notation than do other instruments, but Notion also supports techniques that are specific to other instruments in both notation and playback. With the new cross-staff beaming tool, Notion can now produce quality piano and harp scores. A little planning goes a long way in saving you time. Always look over a score to see places that require some thought and look for opportunities to use cut and paste, which is always the fastest entry method. While NTempo can produce a flowing tempo and is the best choice for live performance, for playback or export purposes, a similar effect can be obtained more quickly by using tempo changes with ritards and accelerandos.

Now that you have completed this chapter, you should know how to do the following:

- Copy and paste to streamline your workflow
- Adjust beams including cross-staff beams
- Add pedaling marks
- Create grace notes
- Change clefs
- Use tempo changes to create a fluid performance
- Apply performance techniques to other instruments

Chapter **11**
THE JAZZ
ENSEMBLE

As we have seen, notation and performance are often two very different things. That is even more evident in jazz. Composers and arrangers have a wide array of shortcuts that make writing faster and are clearly understood by performers. In some cases, these shortcuts result in a better performance than would occur had the music been notated exactly. This presents a problem for notation programs that generally only play what you write, not what you mean. But with Notion, you can have both great playback and notation.

Project Overview

Writing for jazz ensembles involves different articulations and performance techniques. Many arrangers use notation programs for engraving, preferring to work out their ideas on paper. This is a perfectly acceptable way to work. But in this project, we will look at writing music directly into Notion. We'll start with the lead sheet from the online media files and use that as the basis for our arrangement.

Our goal isn't just efficiency, but transparency. We don't want the program to interfere with creativity. Fortunately, Notion not only doesn't interfere; it also makes it easier to write.

By this point, you should be fairly familiar with Notion's palettes, commands, and shortcuts. In this project, you will get a feel for a workflow that is a little less rigid and will jump around a little, just as an arranger might do. It's still efficient, but things are presented as they might occur to the arranger, not the copyist. Although we're just doing a small ensemble, everything here will be applicable to larger bands as well.

The completed chart "Way_Cool_Chart.pdf" is included as a PDF in the online media files. Use that as your reference. If you have two monitors, just place it on one and Notion on the other. If you only have one, you can switch between the PDF and Notion by typing ⌘ + Tab / Ctrl + Tab.

This project can be completed using Notion's basic sample set, but if you are going to do a lot of jazz arranging, you may find that the Jazz Expansion bundle will be worth purchasing.

New Topics	New Shortcuts	
• Copy between files • D.S., coda • Jazz articulations • Custom rehearsal letters • Edit swing control • Hide articulations • Cue notes • Change notehead • Concert score • Re-pitching • Stemless slash notation • Edit drum patterns • Custom chord diagrams • Recent chord list • Drum notation • Attach audio • Clear special • Copy chord symbols • Live Performance commands	Shift + R	Palette 1: Rehearsal Letters
	9999	Palette 8: Breath Mark
	⌘ + Tab / Ctrl + Tab	Cycle open programs
	7	Palette 10: D.S.
	77	Palette 10: Coda
	777	Palette 10: To Coda
	77777777	Palette 10: D.S. al Coda
	o	Palette 6: o (open)
	Shift + = (+)	Palette 6: + (closed)
	x	Palette 3: Noteheads

Table 11-1. New topics and shortcuts.

Basic Procedure

1. Set up the score, including measures, form, repeats, and rehearsal letters.
2. Copy the melody from the lead sheet to the score.
3. Set the tempo and swing feel.
4. Edit the melody to improve the performance quality.
5. Add written articulations.
6. Record a walking bass line.
7. Add the background horn lines.
8. Add the guitar with custom diagrams.
9. Add the written drum part.
10. Add the sounding drum part.
11. Add the piano part.
12. Copy, paste, and complete the intro and coda.
13. Copy and paste the solo section.
14. Attach an audio file for the piano.
15. Finishing touches—dynamics, credits, hiding staves, setting staves to Tacet.
16. Lay out the score.
17. Lay out the parts.

Step by Step

Score Setup

- Select New Score from the Startup window or Choose File > New (⌘ + N / Ctrl + N).
- Add the following instruments (if you have the jazz bundle, use the jazz instruments):
  - trumpet
  - trombone
  - tenor saxophone
  - piano

- acoustic guitar
- upright bass
- drum set
- Drag the instruments so they are in the order listed.
- Click the Track Setup gear for each instrument and change the names and abbreviations. Show only the notation staff for the guitar.
- Click Exit Score Setup or press Esc.
- Type Shift + K (Palette 9: Key Signatures).
- Set Key to B♭ Major.
- Click in the first measure.

Form

It's a good idea before you start writing to make some decisions about the form. This will be a simple head arrangement: one chorus arranged for the horns and one (open) chorus of solos with first and second endings, plus an intro and a tag ending.

Introduction	4 bars
Head	32 bars
Solos	32 + 1 bars
Coda	8 bars

Table 11-2. Arrangement form.

Set Up the Form

This arrangement will be a total of 77 measures. You could type I (Palette 10: Barline) and click in the last measure repeatedly until you have enough measures. But there's a better way. By default, Notion creates scores with 33 measures. The song is in standard AABA form, 8 measures per section for a total of 32 bars. This works out very well for our purposes. We can set up the form and then duplicate it to create our score.

Set the Measures per System

- Choose Score > Full Score Options.
- Select the Layout tab.
- Set Measures per system to 4.

Add Measures for the Introduction

- Type I (Palette 10: Barline).
- Click in the first measure four times.

Add Double Barlines

- Type I I (Palette 10: Double Barline).
- Click in mm. 4, 12, 20, and 28.

Duplicate Empty Measures

When using Duplicate or Copy and Paste with empty measures, it's important to have at least one measure beyond the selection to be copied.

- Double-click m. 5, Shift-click m. 36.
- Type ⌘ + D / Ctrl + D (Edit > Duplicate).

We still need the eight measures for the tag, but duplicating the last eight measures won't quite work. One more measure needs to be added first. Otherwise, while the coda will have eight measures, the previous section will have only seven.

- Type I (Palette 10: Barline).
- Click in the last measure.
- Double-click m. 61, Shift-click m. 68.
- Type ⌘ + D / Ctrl + D (Edit > Duplicate).

Add Repeats and Endings
- Type Shift + ; ; [semicolon] (Palette 10: Forward Repeat).
- Click in m. 37.
- Type Shift + ; (Palette 10: Backward Repeat).
- Click in m. 68.
- Type Shift + ; ; ; (Palette 10: Endings).
- Click in m. 68.

Rehearsal Letters
Adding in rehearsal letters now will ensure we don't lose our place in the score, both while writing and playing the chart.
- Type Shift + R (Palette 1: Rehearsal Letter).
- Click in m. 5. The rehearsal letter A will appear.
- Click in m. 13 and immediately type "A9."
- Click in m. 21. Type "A17."
- Click in m. 29. Type "A25."
- Enter the rehearsal letters B, B9, B17, and B25 in the second chorus.

Signs and Codas
- After the solos, the head will be repeated and will jump to the coda for the tag ending. We use D.S. and Coda signs to do this. Both use the same shortcut, the 7 key.
- Type 7 (Palette 10: D.S.).
- Click in m. 5.
- Type 77 (Palette 10: Coda).
- Click in m. 70.
- Type 777 (Palette 10: To Coda).
- Click the right barline of m. 32.
- Type 7777777 (the 7 key, seven times) (Palette 10: D.S. al Coda).
- Click the right barline of m. 69.

Concert or Transposed Score
Jazz ensemble scores are often in concert pitch rather than showing instruments transposed. Notion has two options for concert scores, *concert pitch*, where the actual pitch is displayed on all tracks, and *concert tuning*, where all octave transpositions have been applied. For this example, use concert tuning. Choose View > Concert Tuning.

▶ Open "Way_Cool-form.notion" to begin here.

Copy the Head
The notes for the head (melody) have already been entered in the lead sheet and we can copy and paste them directly into our arrangement. But first, it's decision time again. Let's put the melody of the A section in the trumpet and the melody of the B section in tenor sax.

▶ The file "Way_Cool-articulations.notion" is a lead sheet with all the performance articulations added. You can use this to replace the head in your chart if you prefer.

Copying Between Two Notion Files

- Open the file "Way_CoolLS.notion."
- Select m. 1 through the second ending (m. 10).
- Type ⌘ + C / Ctrl + C (Edit > Copy).
- Type ⌘ + ` / Ctrl + ` to switch to the arrangement score window.
- Double-click m. 5 of the trumpet part.
- Type ⌘ + V / Ctrl + V (Edit > Paste).
- Type ⌘ + ` / Ctrl + ` to switch to the lead sheet window.
- Select mm. 11–18.
- Type ⌘ + C / Ctrl + C (Edit > Copy).
- Type ⌘ + ` / Ctrl + ` to switch to the arrangement score window.
- Double-click m. 15 of the tenor sax part.
- Type ⌘ + V / Ctrl + V (Edit > Paste).

The last A is the same as the second A. Copy measures 5–10 of the trumpet part and paste it into measure 23. Then copy the two measures of the second ending and paste into measure 29. The double barlines and repeats should make these easy to locate.

Set the Tempo and Swing Feel

Now that the melody has been entered, it's a good time to set the tempo and swing feel. The piece is in a cool jazz style, so a medium-up tempo of about 160 bpm should work well. It should also have a nice smooth swing feel to it, not too bouncy. The swing feel can be set from 0 (straight eighths) to 90 (almost no upbeat), with 25 being the standard triplet feel. The modern swing sound is a little straighter than that, so we'll adjust it a bit closer to even eighths.

- Double-click the metronome marking.
- Change the tempo to "q=160."
- Type Shift + G (Swing Control).
- Click on the first beat of m. 1.
- Double-click the Swing marking.
- Set the swing to 18.

Swing Performance Techniques

Notion does a good job of producing a nice swing feel automatically. But it can sound quite a bit more authentic by simulating some important swing performance techniques.

One key to a good swing feel is a technique called back-accenting. This is where the upbeats in a string of eighth-notes are accented slightly and often slurred into the downbeats, which are often slightly detached. The simplest method is to place accents (>) on the upbeats. Then add slurs from the upbeat to the downbeat. But since all of these are really assumed by the player, they don't need to print, so we'll hide them before later adding the printed articulations. Use the file "Way_Cool-articulations.pdf" as a guide.

- Type 5 (Palette 4: >).
- Click on the upbeat of each pair of consecutive eighth-notes.
- Type Shift + S (Palette 4: Slurs).
- Click on each accented note, then click the next note.
- Select the entire part, right-click and choose Attachments > Hide.

The other important element is the duration of notes. Those back-accented notes need to overlap slightly into the downbeats, and the downbeats should be slightly detached at this tempo. In addition, quarter-notes, particularly upbeat quarter-notes, are usually short, but not quite staccato. The Sequencer Overlay (TAB) can be used to adjust the length of each individual note in the same way one does in the piano-roll view of a DAW. This can be rather tedious as there are no shortcuts, so don't overdo it. Use your ears rather than your eyes. If a note is too long, or an attack of a slurred note too pronounced, it can be worth the effort.

Figure 11-1. Sequencer Overlay.

Click the gray bar (gray indicates the default velocity) and drag left or right to change the duration without changing the written note. You can also click on the notehead and drag left or right to change the starting time of the note. This can be quite useful in passages where copy and paste have been used to create unison or soli sections and where randomizing isn't appropriate.

Written Articulations

Now that the performance aspects have been added and hidden, the articulations that are expected on the written part can be entered. Jazz players use a strong accent (^) or marcato to indicate a slightly accented and shortened note. Type 6 (Palette 4: ^) and click on all upbeat quarter-notes, including those tied between beats 2 and 3, and on upbeat eighth-notes that end a phrase. Type 5 (Palette 4: > [accent]) and click on upbeat dotted quarters. Press Play and listen. You may find you need to go back to Sequencer Overlay and shorten some of the upbeat quarters.

The Rhythm Section

The instruments of the rhythm section can be written in any order, and one or more could have been done earlier in our arrangement. It's important to consider the level of the players for whom you are writing. Younger players, such as the ones for which this piece is intended, will require more specific instructions, whereas advanced players mostly need information about what the rest of the ensemble is doing. In any case, the rhythm section parts will rarely be played exactly as they are written, with the possible exception of the bass, which we will enter now.

The Bass

The bass part can be anything from a specific line to chord changes and slashes similar to the guitar and piano. For younger players, provide a suggested bass line, but give the chord changes, too, to allow more advanced players the freedom to play their own lines.

Depending on your abilities, you might want to enter the bass in real time, in step-time, or even using the mouse. For the most part, we will be entering quarter-notes, so my recommendation is step-time. You can either use the bass line provided online ("Way_Cool_Bass_Line.pdf") or enter one of your choosing. Regardless of the method you use for entry, you will want to accent beats 2 and 4 slightly. You do this in real time by playing those beats a little harder. In step-time, add the accent (5) on those beats during entry.

Once the bass notes have been entered, select all the measures of the bass part (⌘-Shift + A / Ctrl-Shift + A), right-click, and choose Attachments > Hide.

Background Parts

Now that we have the melody and the bass line along with the basic chords, it's time to add the background parts. Once again, making a few basic decisions first will help this along. For this arrangement, the A section has guide tone backgrounds, mainly thirds and sevenths of the chord, that were then changed to support the melody rhythmically. The tenor sax melody in the B section is much busier, so the guide tone backgrounds continue but with less rhythmic variation. For the final A section, the backgrounds join the melody in a three-part soli.

Section	Melody	Backgrounds
A1	Trumpet	2-part rhythmic guidetones
A9	Trumpet	2-part rhythmic guidetones
A17 (bridge)	Tenor sax	2-part static guidetones
A25	Trumpet	3-part soli with trumpet
Solo B section	Tenor sax solo	2-part backgrounds

Table 11-3. The horn background parts.

Once again, you can enter the lines given in the example or write your own. When writing these lines, I mainly used the mouse with shortcuts. When writing directly to Notion, this is the closest thing to pencil and paper. But there are some tricks that will make this even quicker than pencil, too.

Figure 11-2. Tenor sax background line.

Background—Letter A

Enter the tenor line first, using your preferred method.

Re-pitching

The trombone will play the same rhythm as the tenor sax, so rather than enter the notes from scratch, we can copy the tenor part and paste it into the trombone part, then change only the pitches using step-time recording.

- Copy and paste mm. 5–12 from the tenor sax to the trombone.
- Type ⌘ + E / Ctrl + E (Toolbar: Step-time Record).
- Click the first note in the trombone part.
- Play the new pitch (G). Do not select a note value shortcut!
- When you come to a rest, click the next note to skip over it.

Figure 11-3. Trombone background line.

Backgrounds—Letter A9

Use the same process as was used in Letter A. Delete the extra notes in the trombone part. You can do this in Edit mode with the mouse.

Figure 11-4. Tenor sax and trombone backgrounds, letter A9.

Backgrounds—Letter A17

In a big band, this would probably be scored as a sax soli, but with the smaller group, it's best to continue the backgrounds as in A9, but with less rhythmic activity. Use the same process as in the earlier sections. Enter the trumpet part, then copy the line to the trombone and re-pitch as before.

Figure 11-5. Trumpet and trombone backgrounds, letter A17.

Backgrounds—Letter A25

In section A25 we will do a three-part soli. As all three instruments will for the most part play the same rhythm, once again copy and paste the lines and re-pitch, using step-time recording.

Figure 11-6. The three-part soli.

▶ Open "Way_Cool-horns.notion" to begin here.

The Guitar Part

Young guitarists often have trouble with jazz chords, so we'll use the fretboard to add custom chord diagrams to make it a little easier. The "Freddie Green" orchestral style, with four quarter-notes for most measures and an accent on 2 and 4, will work here fine.

Enter Rhythm Slashes

Figure 11-7. Guitar rhythm pattern.

- Enter four quarter-notes with articulations (Figure 11-7) on the open second (B) string.
- Right-click and choose Notes > Show as Rhythm Slash.
- Type ⌘ + D / Ctrl + D (Edit > Duplicate) throughout the first chorus (mm. 6–36).
- Use double-click/Shift-click to select mm. 6–36 (all but m. 5).
- Right-click and choose Notes > Hide Stem.
- Right-click and choose Attachments > Hide.
- Type K (Palette 1: Text).
- Click above m. 2 and type "simile."

> ❶ **TIP:** Try duplicating more than one measure at time.

Creating Custom Chord Diagrams

You can create just about any chord symbol by typing directly into the score or with the Chord Library, but only those for which the library has a diagram will play back correctly (without notating the chord on the staff). The library only has basic forms and doesn't have a lot of good jazz voicings, so we will need to create them by using the blank diagram and the virtual fretboard. The chords are shown Figure 11-8. Now enter the first chord.

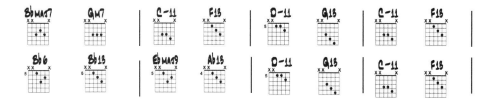

Figure 11-8. Chord diagrams—A section.

- Click the Fretboard button in the Toolbar.
- Choose Palette 1: Chord Diagrams.
- Click beat 1, m. 5.
- Type the chord name (Bbmaj7).
- Click the notes on the fretboard. Make sure you change the open strings to muted.
- Enter the next three chords (complete the first two measures).
- Press Esc.
  Custom chord diagrams will transpose just like notes.
- Double-click m. 6.
- Type ⌘ + D / Ctrl + D twice (Edit > Duplicate).
- Double-click m. 7.
- Right-click and choose Tools > Transpose.
- Set the transposition to Major, Second, Up.
- Press Return/Enter.

Now create diagrams for measures 9 and 10 and press Esc. Measures 11 and 12 are the same as measures 7 and 8, so copy and paste them.

> **! TIP:** It's very easy to enter custom chord diagrams where you don't want them, so until you get the hang of them, it's a good idea to press Esc after you enter one. If you enter one incorrectly, click the diagram in your score and correct it, rather than delete it. This will help keep your Recent Chord list clean.

- Click the Recent Chord tab in the Chord Library.
- Select the C11 chord diagram.
- Click on beat 1, m. 8.
- Select the F13 chord diagram.
- Click on beat 3, m. 8.

Guitar—Rehearsal Letter A9

The chords for the first six measures of A9 are the same as in the A. Copy and paste the first six measures to A9 (m. 13). The last two measures of this section are a little different, but only one chord is new. As the Bb6 has already been created, it can be selected from the Recent Chord list.

All of the chords used in your piece, including the custom diagrams you created, are stored in the Recent Chord list. You can select any chord from the list to use in your chart.

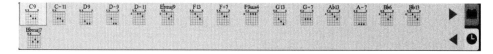

Figure 11-9. The Recent Chord list.

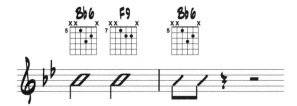

Figure 11-10. Guitar—Measures 19 and 20.

- Select both measures.
- Choose Edit > Clear.
- Type H (Palette 3: Half-Note).
- Click twice in m. 19.
- Type E (Palette 3: Eighth-Note).
- Click twice in m. 20.
- Select both measures, right-click, and choose Notes > Show as Rhythm Slash.
- Add the B♭6 chords from the Recent Chord list.
- Create a new custom diagram for the F9 chord.

Guitar—Rehearsal Letter A17

We can use the Recent Chord list and Transpose feature to add all but the first and last chords in this section.

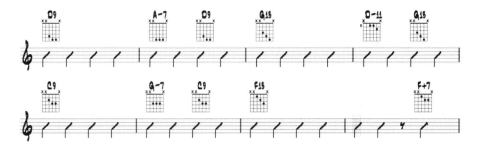

Figure 11-11. Guitar—the bridge.

- Create a custom diagram for the D9 on beat 1, m. 22.
- Select G7 from the Recent Chord list.
- Click beat 1, m. 23.
- Double-click m. 23.
- Right-click and choose Tools > Transpose.
- Set the transposition to Major, Second, Up.
- Press Return/Enter.
  Enter the chords for next two measures, G13 and D11, from the Recent Chord list.
- Select D9 from the Recent Chord list and enter on beat 1, m 26.
- Double-click m. 26.
- Right-click and choose Tools > Transpose.

- Set the transposition to Major, Second, Down (C9).
- Press Return/Enter.
- Enter F13 from the Recent Chord list.
- Create the custom diagram for F+7.

Guitar—Rehearsal Letter A25

The last A section is identical to the second A. Copy the eight measures of A9 and paste into A25.

> ❶ **TIP:** Export the guitar track as a Standard MIDI File. Now import that file and you will have a part with all of the voicings written in standard notation.

▶ Open "Way_Cool-guitar.notion" to begin here.

The Written Drum Part

We will be creating two drum parts: one for playback and a written part for the drummer. Providing specific drum beats for a drummer in this type of ensemble will only cause a stiff and unmusical performance. However, for playback purposes, we'll need a part that swings.

The written part consists mainly of slashes, with occasional hits and fill instructions. The hits are shown either as cue notes on the top of the staff (section cues) or as full-size notes on the middle line staff (ensemble cues). You can assume a drummer will punctuate phrases, so only indicate fills where you want them to really play, in this case, measures 27 and 28 and later in the coda.

The slashes are entered in voice 2.

- Type ⌘ + 2 / Ctrl + 2 (Palette 3: Voice 2).
- Type Q.
- Enter four quarter-notes on the middle line in m. 5.
- Double-click the measure.
- Right-click and choose Notes > Show as Rhythm Slash.
- Right-click and choose Notes > Hide Stem.
- Duplicate or copy/paste through the entire piece.

> ❶ **TIP:** Duplicate eight measures, one at a time, and then select and duplicate eight measures at a time.

The Cue notes are in voice 1 and are there to give the drummer information about what the rest of the band is playing. As the form is AABA, we only need enter the cues once for the A section. Only type the rests and notes that are needed; don't fill out entire measures unless that's information the drummer needs.

- Type ⌘ + 1 / Ctrl + 1 (Palette 3: Voice 1).
- Measure 6: Enter an eighth-rest (EE) and dotted quarter-note (QD).
- Measure 7: Enter a dotted quarter (QD) and eighth-note (E), dotted quarter-rest (QQD), and eighth-note (E). Add a tie to the last note (Shift + T).
- Measure 8: Enter a dotted quarter (QD) and eighth-note (E).
- Measures 9 and 10: Enter an eighth-rest (EE) and eighth-note (E).
- Measures 11 and 12: Enter an eighth-rest, quarter-note, eighth-note, and half-rest.
- Add a tie to the last note in mm. 11 and 12.
- Click/Shift-click the half-rests in mm. 11 and 12.
- Right-click and choose Rests > Hide Rests.

- Select mm. 6–10.
- Right-click and choose Select Special > Select Voice 1.
- Right-click and choose Notes > Set as Cue Notes.
- Type ⌘ + C / Ctrl + C (Edit > Copy).
- Double-click m. 14.
- Right-click and choose Paste Special > Paste into Voice 1.
- Double-click m. 30.
- Right-click and choose Paste Special > Paste into Voice 1.

Measures 19 and 20

There are a couple of measures to edit manually. There's a fill in measure 19 and both ensemble and section cues in measure 20. You can do this in Edit mode.

- Make sure you are in voice 2 (⌘ + 2 / Ctrl + 2).
- Select beat 1, m. 20 and delete it.
- Type E and enter two eighth-notes on the middle line on beat 1.
- Type 6 and add a ^ (strong accent) to the second eighth-note.
- Select Voice 1 (⌘ + 1 / Ctrl + 1).
- Type HH and enter a half-rest in m. 20.
- Type EE and enter an eighth-rest.
- Type QD and enter the dotted quarter.
- Select the half-rest.
- Right-click and choose Rests > Hide.
- Type K (Palette 1: Text).
- Click on beat 1, m. 19 and type "Fill."

Measure 28

Type E and enter four eighth-notes in voice 1.

Measure 36

- Copy m. 20 and paste into m. 36.
- Delete the cue notes in voice 1.

  Cue notes are shown in gray and don't print by default, so they need to be set to print.

- Choose Score > Full Score Options.
- Select the More tab.
- Tick "Print Cue Notes."

  Now set the part to Tacet.

- Click anywhere in the drum staff.
- Select the whole part (⌘-Shift + A / Ctrl-Shift + A).
- Right-click and choose Notes > Set as Tacet.

The Sounding Drum Part

The sounding drum part will be placed on a new drumset staff that will be hidden once it's done.

- Type ⌘ + T / Ctrl + T (Score > Score Setup).
- Add a drumset instrument.
- Rename it Drums (play).
- Drag the staff to the bottom of the score.
- Click the Eye icon of the original drum part to hide the staff.

As we've seen in Chapter 5, the virtual drumpad also includes a library of drum grooves that we can use as the basis for our drum part. If you created the library files, open that.

We'll start with one of the basic patterns and do some modifications to it along the way. We'll also throw in a few fills and record some parts as well. This won't take too long and it's worth the time when playback is important.

The Basic Groove ("Four on the Floor") A and A9

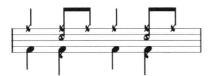

Figure 11-12. The basic groove.

- Select "Jazz 8ths 3" and click in m. 5.
- Press Esc.
- Type ⌘ + 2 / Ctrl + 2 (Palette 3: Voice 2).
- Type Q (Palette 3: Quarter-Note).
- Add bass drum hits on beats 2 and 4; duplicate (⌘ + D / Ctrl + D) through m. 7.
- Select mm. 5–10 of the drum part.
- Copy and paste into m. 13.

Basic Groove Variation A25

A variation for the last A section will round out the arrangement.

Figure 11-13. Basic groove variation.

- Place "Jazz 8ths 3" in m. 29.
- Type E and replace the side sticks with snare drum hits on beats 2 and 4.
- Duplicate to fill mm. 29–35.

Bridge—The Comping Snare

Adding a little more variety to the basic groove by varying the snare and ride cymbal, using the virtual drumpad, will help set the bridge apart from the A sections.

Entering Drum Hits

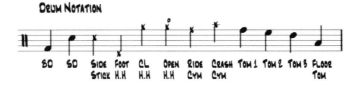

Figure 11-14. Drum notation.

Drum hits can be entered using the mouse, virtual drumpad, or a MIDI device. While drums use a neutral clef, for note entry purposes it works as treble clef. It's common notation practice for cymbals to use the x notehead; however, by default, the virtual drumpad will enter all notes with standard noteheads. As the drum part will be hidden eventually, this won't be a problem. The side stick snare, on the other hand, requires a circle x notehead to trigger the correct sample.

Now enter a varied ride and snare drum pattern. The ride should be mainly on the downbeats with occasional upbeats. Add one or two snare drum hits on just about any beat; just change it up each measure. If this seems too daunting, then use the pattern shown in the score, but know that that one is essentially an improvisation.

- Copy m. 5 and paste into m. 21.
- Double-click m. 21.
- Right-click and choose Select Special > Select Voice 1.
- Choose Edit > Clear.
- Duplicate (⌘ + D / Ctrl + D) for a total six measures.
- Type ⌘ + 1 / Ctrl + 1 or click the V1 button on the virtual drum.
- Type ⌘ + E / Ctrl + E or click the Step-time Record button in the Transport.
- Click on m. 21.
- Enter snare and ride cymbals for the next six measures.

Fills

We'll put fills every four measures to help delineate the form. The fills from the library are a start but will require a few modifications.

Measures 8 and 16

Figure 11-15. Fill measures 8 and 16.

- Change the hi-hat on beat 3 to an eighth-note (=E).
- Add snare drum hits (not side sticks) on the + of 3 and beat 4.
- Type ⌘ + 2 / Ctrl + 2 (Palette 3: Voice 2).
- Change the bass drum on beat 4 to two eighth-notes.
- Copy m. 8 and paste into m. 16.

Measure 12

Figure 11-16. Drum fill measure 12.

- Select "Jazz Fill 1."
- Click in m. 12. It will overwrite the existing measure.
- Type Q (Palette 3: Quarter-Note).
- Enter a bass drum on beats 1 and 4.
- Enter a snare on beat 4.

Measures 19, 20, 27, and 28

Figure 11-17. Drum fill measure 32.

- Select "Jazz Fill 9."
- Click in m. 19.
- Click in m. 27.

Measure 32

- Select "Jazz Fill 1."
- Click in m. 32.
- Select the first two beats of the fill and copy it (⌘ + C / Ctrl + C).
- Click on beat 3 of m. 32 and paste (⌘ + V / Ctrl + V).

Measure 36
Copy m. 28 and paste into m. 36.

Piano

The piano has a similar issue as the drums in that the sounding part and the written part are not really the same. You can employ the same method as we did with the drums, creating separate parts for each, and then recording a piano part either in real time or constructing it with step-time recording or even mouse/keyboard entry. For now, because the guitar is already playing the chords, we'll use copy and paste to fill out the part. The Pages Across view will make it a little easier to copy the chords, as we'll work page by page. We can also add the changes to the bass part at the same time.

- Choose View > Pages Across.
- Select and copy a measure of slashes (without cues) from the drum part.
- Paste into m. 5.
- Duplicate to fill out the entire arrangement.
- Beginning at m. 5, click/Shift-click to select the chords on that page from the trumpet track.
- Copy the selected chords and paste into m. 5 of the piano and bass parts.
- Continue working page by page through m. 20.
- From mm. 21 to 28, type Shift + C and enter the chords (or copy/paste if you prefer).
- Copy the chords from the trumpet part from measures 29–36 and paste into the piano and bass parts.

A measure can have both slashes and notes.

- Delete the slashes on beats 2–4, m. 20.
- Manually enter the notes.

The last measure of the chorus (m. 36) has all instruments ending on two eighth-notes.

- Copy the measure from any of the other instruments and paste it into the piano part.
- If necessary, select and right-click the measure and choose Notes > Show as Rhythm Slash.
- Type Shift + C and enter the chord symbol.

▶ Open "Way_Cool-drums.notion" to begin here.

Clearing Chord Symbols

The chord symbols in the trumpet and tenor sax parts during the melody aren't needed any longer. We can easily strip those out using the Clear Special command.

- Click anywhere in the trumpet staff.
- Type ⌘-Shift + A / Ctrl-Shift + A (Edit > Select Part).
- Shift-click the tenor sax part.
- Right-click and choose Edit > Clear Special.
- Tick "Chord Symbols" and "Tempo Marks."
- Press Return/Enter or click OK.

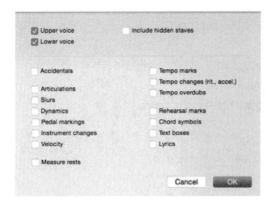

Figure 11-18. The Clear Special dialog window.

Solo Section

Most of the solo section can be created by copy and pasting from the A chorus. Then, to make it a little more realistic for practicing, we'll attach an audio file for the piano comping.

- Select and copy the guitar and bass parts mm. 5–36.
- Double-click the guitar m. 37 and paste (⌘ + V / Ctrl + V).
- Select and copy the piano part mm. 5–36.
- Paste into m. 37 of the trumpet, tenor sax, trombone, and piano.
- Copy m. 68 and paste into m. 69.
- Select and copy the "real" drum part mm. 21–26.
- Paste into m. 37 of the "real" drum part.
- Duplicate (⌘ + D / Ctrl + D) four times.

  For the written drum part, we'll use an arranging shortcut.
- Type K (Palette 1: Text).
- Click in the first measure of letter B.
- Type "PLAY 8."
- In the font dialog, set the size to 18.
- Copy the text.
- Paste at B9, B17, and B25.

  Now attach the audio file to the piano staff. Notion only supports CD-quality (16-bit, 44.1 kHz) .wav files.
- Choose Score > Attach Audio.
- Select file "riddimpiano.wav" from the online files.

Introduction and Coda

▶ Open the file "Way_Cool-intro.notion" online. You can copy and paste most of the following sections from this file.

The introduction uses a dominant pedal point for the rhythm section and borrows a rhythmic idea from the song for the horns. The written and real drum parts are the same, using open and closed hi-hats. Enter them now.

Figure 11-19. Drums—introduction.

- Type x (Palette 3: x Notehead).
- Type Q (Palette 3: Quarter-Note).
- Enter notes (G) through beat 1, m. 4.
- Type E (Palette 3: Eighth-Note).
- Enter two eighth-notes on beat 2.
- Type E (Palette 3: Eighth-Rest).
- Type x repeatedly (five times) until the regular notehead appears.
- Type QD (Palette 3: Dotted Quarter).
- Enter B (middle line).
- Type o (Palette 6: o).
- Click on beats 1 and 3 in the intro.
- Type Shift + = (Palette 6: +).
- Click on beats 2 and 4 and the last eighth-note in the intro.

The coda uses a variation on a tag ending, where two measures are repeated twice, followed by a drum fill and a final "stinger" chord. Most of this was done by copying and pasting from other sections of the arrangement. Copy the coda measures from the file and paste into measure 70. You'll then change a couple of notes in the piano and guitar, add the drum fill, and finish with the stinger.

Figure 11-20. The stinger.

- Type Shift + C (Palette 1: Chord Symbol) and enter the chord C/B♭ over the last chord in the piano and guitar parts.
- Open the Drum Library.
- Select "Jazz Fill 11."
- Double-click the last measure.
- Copy and paste into m. 76 (the previous).
- Enter the last measure with the mouse.
- Enter the slashes for the written part.
- Type / / / [slash, three times] (Palette 6: Unmeasured Tremolo).
- Click on the last note.
- Type K and add the text "Fill" to m. 76.

- Enter the dynamics ("f") and the fermata ("9").
- Fermatas should be above the note. Click-drag them, if necessary.
- Click-drag chord symbols, dynamics, and fermatas as needed to avoid collisions.

Finishing Touches

Dynamics

There aren't a lot of dynamic markings in this score. For playback purposes, setting the background parts one level lower than the melody will produce better results. The *forte* samples for the jazz horns are very bright. This works well for big bands, but is a little too much for this cool style, so don't use more than *mezzo forte* until the very end.

Credits

There are some final things to take care of. First, add the title, composer, and copyright information. (If you are using my example, thank you for that.) Now open Full Score Options and select the Fonts tab. Set Copyright to TTkJazzTextExtended.

Fill with Rests

Rests need to be filled in for all parts except the written drum part.
- Type ⌘ + A / Ctrl + A.
- ⌘-click / Ctrl-click the drum staff.
- Right-click anywhere and choose Tools > Fill with Rests.

Hide Staves

The "real" drum part is only for playback, so it needs to be hidden from the score. Even though hidden it will still play back.
- Type ⌘ + T / Ctrl + T (Score > Score Setup).
- Click the Eye icon for the real drum part.
- Click Exit Score Setup (Esc).

Bracket and Barline Groups

The drum part that was added was not automatically included in the bracket group.
- Type ⌘ + A / Ctrl + A (Edit > Select All).
- Right-click and choose Staff Groups > Make Bracket Group.
- Right-click and choose Staff Groups > Make Barline Group.

Set Piano to Tacet

Most of the piano part should not play back. We could mute the tracks in the mixer, but it's best to set it to Tacet.
- Click in the piano staff.
- Type ⌘-Shift + A / Ctrl-Shift + A (Edit > Select Part).
- Right-click and choose Notes > Set as Tacet.
- Select mm. 1–4 in the piano part.
- Right-click and choose Notes > Set as Tacet (to deselect).
- Select m. 20.
- Right-click and choose Notes > Set as Tacet (to deselect).

Layout

Combo scores can be displayed in portrait view, but often a better choice is to use landscape view. With a score such as this there's really no way to create a perfectly uniform score from page to page. Just keep in mind, Notion isn't really an engraving program. Look at each page individually and make decisions that ensure each page is functional on its own.

For this score, start with these basic settings:

- US Letter: Landscape.
- Top margin: 1.25.
- Top margin, first page: 2.

This should give you a pretty balanced view. But because so much space is available, we might as well use some and increase the space between the staves.

- Choose Score > Full Score Options.
- Select the More tab.
- Set Staff Spacing to 2 (or even 3, if you prefer).

The last step is to move some measures around. Go through the score and look for measures that might be better on the next system. For example, let's start the coda on a new system.

- Double-click/right-click the first measure of the coda.
- Choose Measure 70 > Force New System.

Go through the piece and look for any other places where this might improve the look or readability.

Figure 11-21. Context menu: Force New System.

There is no reliable way to force a measure to move to the previous system. Link to Next Measure will make a decision on which system the linked measures will appear. Most of the time, it's pretty clear which way they will have to go, as Notion will not allow you to overcrowd a system.

Parts

As we saw in Chapter 8, the parts will not require a lot of editing.

- Choose Score > Parts Options.
- Select the Layout tab.
- Set Titles on first system to "None."
- Set Titles following to "None."

As we did with the score, move measures around to help with readability. The coda should start on a new system.

Finally, you'll need to drag the chord symbols below the ending brackets and align them with the other chords on that line. Click/Shift-click the chords. Right-click and choose Chords > Align Chord Symbols.

Next Step: Rehearsal Scores

We've looked at exporting audio for use as backing tracks for practice, but there are some ways to use the Notion file itself, too, using some of the special Live Performance mode shortcuts. You can also use a MIDI keyboard to trigger NTempo.

To practice a written part: Open the mixer and mute the track that corresponds to your instrument. Use the shortcuts to quickly navigate to other spots in the song.

To practice soloing: Use the shortcuts shown in Table 11-4 to navigate. Pressing the Return/Enter key anytime while playback is within a repeated section will cause the playback marker to turn orange, and it will take the repeat or first ending until you exit by pressing = [equal sign].

Vamp inside repeat	Return/Enter
Exit repeat	"="
Next rehearsal mark	Shift +]
Previous rehearsal mark	Shift + [
Rewind to previous spot	Delete/Backspace
Rewind to beginning	Delete/Backspace 2 times

Table 11-4. Live Performance shortcuts.

❶ TIP: You can change endings to play as many times as you want. Click the bracket of the first ending and type the total number of times you want the section to repeat. For example, type "3" and the first ending will be labeled "1.2.3." and the last ending, "4."

Summary

Jazz arranging and composition present some unique challenges. The standard notation is interpreted quite differently than in classical music, and arrangers use quite a lot of shorthand techniques that a notation program can't interpret. Using hidden staves and articulations, you can have the best of both worlds: appropriate notation and quality playback.

As you complete this chapter you should know how to do the following:

- Copy music between separate files
- Add signs and codas
- Create realistic jazz performances
- Add measures one at a time and in groups
- Customize rehearsal letters
- Adjust the swing feel
- Set notes as cue notes
- Display the score in concert pitch or tuning
- Enter stemless slash notation
- Change noteheads
- Edit patterns from the Drum Library
- Create custom chord diagrams and reuse them
- Copy and paste chord symbols and diagrams
- Attach audio files to a track
- Control live performance with computer keyboard

Chapter **12**
SCORING TO VIDEO

Writing music for video is made easier with Notion. You can import videos with or without SMPTE timecode, sync the video to the score, assign hit points, and then adjust tempo to fit the music to them. The great playback capabilities make for great mockups to present to your director or client.

Project Overview

In this project, you'll sync a score to a short public-domain video from the National Park Service, showing scenes from Yellowstone Park. Other videos can be found at the Park Service website, at http://www.nps.gov/pub_aff/video/index.html. The video provided online includes SMPTE timecode, though for short videos, it's not really necessary. The process is still the same, for the most part. We'll go through the technical process, but I'll leave the scoring to you.

New Topics	New Shortcuts	
• Attach video • Tap tempo • Mark hit points • VST instruments • VST effects • ReWire	Opt + → / Alt + → (right arrow)	Advance one frame
	Opt + ← / Alt + ← (left arrow)	Rewind one frame
	Opt-Shift + → / Alt-Shift + →	Advance 10 frames
	Opt-Shift + ← / Alt-Shift + ←	Rewind 10 frames
	Shift + O	Assign hit point
	⌘ + ' / Ctrl + ' (apostrophe)	Show/Hide video window

Table 12-1. New topics and shortcuts.

Basic Procedure

1. Create a new score with a basic staff and an NTempo staff.
2. Attach the video and set the frame rate and start times.
3. Find a basic tempo by using Live Performance mode.
4. Mark the hit points.
5. Sync the hit points to the score by using Fit in Time.
6. Adjust tempos.
7. Write the music.

Step by Step

Create a New Score

- Type ⌘ + N / Ctrl + N (File > New).
- Choose Special > Basic Staff.
- Choose Special > NTempo Staff.
- Press Esc.

Attach the Video

- Choose Score > Video Setup.
- Click Attach Video . . . .
- Locate the file "Yellowstone Morning SMPTE.mp4."
- Click OK.
- Set Frame rate to 29.97 NDF (non-drop frame).
- Click OK.

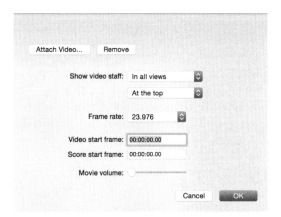

Figure 12-1. Attach Video dialog window.

> **!TIP:** If you are using your own video, you can find the frame rate by opening it in QuickTime and typing ⌘ + I.

Set the Basic Tempo

We'll use Live Performance mode to find a basic tempo. The goal is to find a tempo that will catch most of the hits (scene changes). It's important to understand that tempo and speed of the music are two separate things. You can have a fast tempo with long notes or vice versa, but you don't want the tempo to jump abruptly to an irrational value, as a conductor can't really do that. Double time and other musical tempo changes are fine, but 43 percent faster is a recipe for disaster. There's no one right answer and this might take a few tries before you find a comfortable tempo. We'll need notes in the NTempo track, so enter those first.

Enter NTempo Notes
- Enter four quarter-notes in the NTempo staff.
- Select the measure.
- Type ⌘ + D / Ctrl + D (Edit > Duplicate) and copy it to all measures.

Tap Tempo
- Click the Live Performance Mode button.
- Tap a computer key while watching with the video.
- Try to keep a relatively steady beat and tap when scenes change.
- Watch the Performance HUD to get an idea of the basic starting tempo.
- Double-click the initial tempo mark and change the tempo.

Figure 12-2. The Performance HUD.

Tap tempo indicated that a tempo of around 58–60 would work, so set the initial tempo to 60. This is only one possibility. If you have a different tempo, go right ahead and use it.

Mark the Hit Points
Cues and hits are usually determined in a spotting session between the director and composer. For this short film, we will mark each scene change as a hit. We need to use shortcuts to do this as there are no menu commands. The basic process is to use the shuttle shortcuts to advance the video frame by frame until a cut occurs and then mark the first frame of the new scene as a hit.

Assigning Hits
- Rewind to the beginning.
- Click the video window.
- Press Opt-Shift + → / Alt-Shift + → and hold until the scene changes.
- Type Opt + ← / Alt + ← to rewind one frame at a time until the scene changes back.
- Type Opt + → / Alt + → one frame to the scene change (00:00:14.18).
- Type Shift + O to Assign Hit Point.
- Name the first hit point "Creek."
- Press OK.
  Repeat the process for the remaining hit points as shown in Table 12-2.

	Time	Name
1	00:00:14.18	Creek
2	00:00:31.11	Waterfall
3	00:00:48.20	Sunrise
4	00:00:55.24	Clouds
5	00:01:00.29	Mountain
6	00:01:22.19	Cliff
7	00:01:43.07	End

Table 12-2. Hit points.

Fit Music in Time

Hits should occur in musically precise locations, usually a downbeat or an upbeat, depending on the significance of the hit and the musical context. In this video, hits 1, 3, and 5 are stronger than hits 2, 4, and 6, which are continuations of the previous idea. So hits 1, 3, and 5 should be on downbeats of measures, whereas the other three only need occur in time.

The goal is to adjust the meter and tempo so that the hits occur within plus or minus two frames of a downbeat or upbeat, while avoiding any abrupt tempo changes that aren't metrical, such as half-time. Notion only indicates the time code for the downbeat of each measure, so first adjust the meter prior to any hit that is more than 30 frames from beat 1. Select all the measures from the previous hit to the current one and choose Tools > Fit in Time. Change the end frame time to the hit point time stamp and click OK. If you have a handle on that and want to try it on your own, please do. Otherwise, the hit-by-hit instructions follow.

Hit Point 1: Creek

The first hit point is at 00:00:14.18. At our tempo, it's going to be close to beat 3 of measure 4. We'll need to change the meter first to line up near a downbeat.

Figure 12-3. The Fit in Time dialog window.

- Set the meter in m. 4 to 2/4.
- Set the meter in m. 5 to 4/4.
- Delete two quarter-notes in m. 4.
- Select mm. 1–4.
- Choose Tools > Fit in Time.
- Set End frame to the hit point's location (00:00:14.18).
- Press Tab to calculate the duration.
- Click OK.

The first hit point can be used to set our initial tempo a little more precisely. The indication shows that our tempo should be 4.424 percent slower. A little math (60 times 95.576%, or 0.95576) shows the starting temporary should be 57.346 bpm. Change the tempo and then delete the text "(4.424% slower)." The first hit will now be lined up on the downbeat of measure 5.

Hit Point 2: Waterfall

The second hit, which is a secondary hit, now lines up almost perfectly, so we need do nothing here.

Hit Point 3: Sunrise

At 00:00:48.20, this hit is closer to beat 2 than beat 1. As a primary hit, we need it on a downbeat. We are only trying to line up the hits right now, so we'll change one measure to 5/4. We can always change it later as the music requires.

- Set the meter in m. 12 to 5/4.
- Set the meter in m. 13 to 4/4.
- Add a quarter-note to m. 12.
- Select mm. 9–12.
- Choose Tools > Fit in Time.
- Set End frame to 00:00:48.20.
- Press Tab to calculate the duration.
- Click OK.

Hit Points 4 and 5: Clouds and Mountain

These next two hits occur rather quickly, so it might be a good idea to look at them together. Hit #4 is closer to beat 4 and hit #5 is closer to beat 2, so we'll need to do some meter changes first.

- Set the meter in m. 14 to 3/4.
- Set the meter in m. 15 to 5/4.
- Select mm. 13–15.
- Choose Tools > Fit in Time.
- Set End frame to the hit point time stamp 00:01:00.29.
- Press Tab to recalculate the length.
- Click OK.
  Both hits now line up perfectly.

Hit Point 6: Cliff

This hit is closer to beat 2 now, so we will need to add a beat in one measure.

- Set the meter in m. 22 to 5/4.
- Select mm. 18–22.
- Choose Tools > Fit in Time.
- Set End frame to the hit point time stamp 00:01:22.19 (remember ±2 frames).
- Press Tab to recalculate the length.
- Click OK.

Hit Point 7: End

This isn't actually a hit, but the end of the music must coincide with the end of the cue. Directors can get really upset if the music hangs over. This hit is off by a few frames, but we won't need any meter changes. Because we'll probably be sustaining at the end, we don't need to change the tempo from the last clip; we can just do the last measure.

Delete the Extra Measures

- Select (double-click/Shift-click) m. 27 though the last measure.
- Type ⌘ + X / Ctrl + X (Edit > Cut).

We now have a tempo map synchronized to our film. There are slight tempo changes throughout, gradually pushing the beat a bit, but none would pose a challenge for the conductor. The meter changes we used are only for the purpose of creating the map. Feel free to change them to suit the music you write; as long as you maintain the same number of beats, the music and video will stay in sync. As I said before, for a short project such as this, SMPTE timecode on the video is not actually a necessity. The process would be the same with or without it. The main purpose of the having timecode on the video is to provide points of reference when discussing the music with the director.

The actual composing of music for film is beyond the scope of this book. Much has been written about it and many videos and sites on the Internet are devoted to the subject. We have already addressed the most important aspects: tempo and synchronization. The rest is up to you.

Next Step: VSTis and ReWire

For smaller independent film projects, you may find the budget is such that you are expected to provide the final audio for the film. Unless you have an orchestra waiting in a studio somewhere, this can result in almost as much work as scoring the film in the first place. The built-in playback capabilities of Notion are fine for mockups. But for production audio, you'll probably want to take that one step further and use one of the excellent third-party VST libraries and then mix it in your DAW through the ReWire protocol. Fortunately, Notion provides great support for both.

> **! TIP:** Notion runs in either 64-bit mode (default) or 32-bit mode. Plug-ins must be in a matching mode. If a plug-in won't work with Notion, the first option is to upgrade the plug-in. Otherwise, you will need to restart Notion in 32-bit mode. On the Mac, right-click the app icon and choose Get Info and tick "Open in 32-bit mode." Windows users will need to install the 32-bit version of Notion and use that instead. Of course, your 64-bit plug-ins will not work when Notion is running in 32-bit mode.

VST Instruments and Effects

VST is a plug-in format created by Steinberg that has wide support. Any VST instrument (VSTi) or effect can be used in Notion, but there are a few sample libraries—Vienna Symphonic Library, Garritan Personal Orchestra, East-West Quantum Leap Symphonic Orchestra, Miroslav Philharmonic, LA Scoring Strings, and Virtual Ensemble Trilogy—which have built-in support and respond to articulations, dynamics, and other techniques in virtually the same way as the built-in Notion instruments.

Using VST Plug-ins

- Choose Notion > Plug-in Manager.
- Select the desired library or effect.
- Click Enable.
- Click Close.

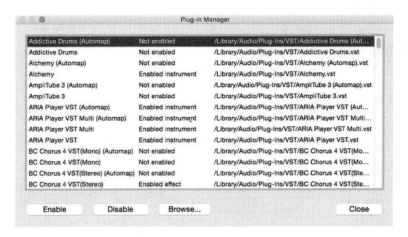

Figure 12-4. Plug-in Manager.

The VST instrument library will now appear in the instrument sets in the Score Setup window and VST effects will be available as inserts in the mixer.

Figure 12-5. VST Libraries in Score Setup.

Multi-channel Tracks

You can assign instruments from any of the supported libraries to tracks in the same way you assign Notion instruments, either by selecting them when the track is created or by using the drop-down menu in the Track Setup dialog box. But for instruments that are not supported, you will need to use a multi-channel track.

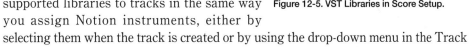

Figure 12-6. VST Effects in the Mixer Insert pop-up menu.

- Type ⌘ + T / Ctrl + T (Score > Score Setup).
- Click on VST Instruments.
- Choose a VSTi from the upper palette.
- From the plug-in interface, assign instruments to a few channels.
- Create one basic staff for each channel in the plug-in.
- Exit Score Setup.
- Click on the first basic staff.
- Choose Tools > Use Instrument.

Figure 12-7. Available VST instruments in Score Setup.

- Tick "Show all Instruments."
- Select the plug-in (not the basic staff).
- Click the Channel drop-down menu.
- Select Channel 1.
- Repeat for additional tracks, assigning them to the next available MIDI channel.

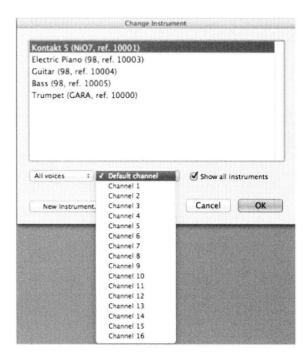

Figure 12-8. The Use Instrument dialog window.

Custom Rules

You can go beyond the capabilities of the built-in instruments by creating custom rules for your external libraries, even the ones with built-in support. This lets you assign MIDI messages and data to any text or graphic expression or take advantage of special features in the library.

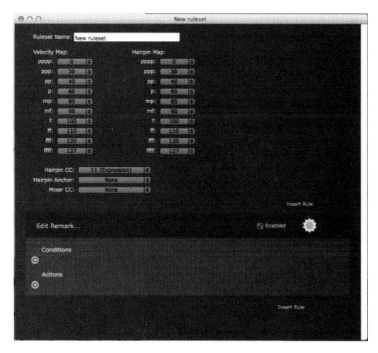

Figure 12-9. The Custom Rules editor.

For the libraries mentioned earlier, that means you can add rules to such dynamics as *fp* or *sfz* to which Notion's own instruments don't respond. For unsupported plug-ins, you'll have to create your own set. Fortunately, a community of custom rule developers post rulesets on the PreSonus Forum that can help get you started, and the new Custom Rules editor lets you create rulesets without having to worry about XML syntax. Nonetheless, this isn't for the faint of heart. You must really understand how your external library works to create a useful ruleset. From there you can choose to import an existing set, edit an existing set, or create a new set. Once you've created a set that works, consider exporting it and posting it on the forum for others to use. For example, let's look at creating a custom rule so instruments will respond to the *forte-piano (fp)* dynamic.

Creating a New Ruleset
- Choose Tools > Use Rules (Shift + Y).
- Click New.
- Name the Ruleset "GPO fp."
- Set Condition to "Technique is on."
- Set Technique to "fp."
- Set Action to "Send CC."
- Set CC # to 1, 7, or 11 (depending on which your library uses for volume).
- Set Value to "40."
- Set Timing to "After note-on."
- Close the Dialog box.
- Type Shift + I.

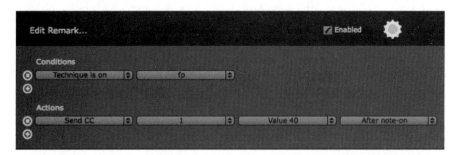

Figure 12-10. Adding rules.

Add the Rule to the Score
- Create a score with any VST instrument.
- Enter a whole note.
- Type 'fp (Palette 4: *fp*).
- Type Shift + Y.
- Click Use.
- Click on the *fp* dynamic.
- Press the spacebar to play.

The Sequencer Staff

Real-time recording into a standard instrument staff only records MIDI note on and off information. For most purposes, that will do fine. But occasionally, you may want to be able to record other MIDI messages, such as the sustain pedal or pitch bend. For this you use a sequencer staff. The sequencer staff only works with VST instruments and is the same as a track in a DAW. It will record all MIDI messages and display them in a piano-roll type display. When you play it back, you will hear the recording exactly as you played it, with all expressions. You can also create a sequencer staff, assign it to an instrument, and overdub any MIDI messages that will affect the notated staff. Sequencer staves can be converted to notation, but only note on and off messages will remain.

To Create a Sequencer Staff
- Type ⌘-Shift + T / Ctrl-Shift + T (Tools > Staff Settings).
- Click the Notation tab.
- Tick the Sequencer Staff checkbox.

To Convert a Sequencer Staff to Notation
- Click in the staff.
- Choose Edit > Select Part.
- Choose Tools > Convert to Notation.

> **❶ TIP:** If you like to record notes and other MIDI messages, such as sustain, mod wheel, pitch bend, and aftertouch, at the same time, create two sequencer staves. Record on one of the staves, then copy and paste it to the other sequencer staff. Convert the second staff to notation. Set the notation to Tacet and hide the sequencer staff.

ReWire

ReWire is a protocol created by Propellerhead that allows one audio/MIDI program, the host, to control another, the slave. Notion can function as either a host or slave. Whichever program is opened first will be the host.

When using Notion as a slave, usually with a DAW, it will essentially function as audio tracks in the DAW. Notion will follow the tempo of the host and processing can be applied. This can be especially useful when using Notion tracks alongside digital audio tracks or using non-VST processors or instruments. One very important thing to know is that, because Notion is following the timing of the host, it will not play repeats, so don't use them in scores that will ultimately be ReWired.

Perhaps the best reason to use Notion as a slave is to apply mixer automation. In that case, set the outputs of each track to a separate output. In the DAW, assign each output to a separate track. You can then treat it as you would an internal audio track. Consult the manual of your DAW for information on how to use ReWire in that program.

The main reason to use Notion as the host is for live performance when you have software instruments that are either not VST instruments or are easier to deal with using another program's tools.

Summary

Synchronizing video to a score is a simple matter using Notion's built-in video tools. NTempo makes it easy to find a base tempo and the shuttle shortcuts let you find hit points quickly and precisely. Notion's built-in instruments will do a great job creating mockups for clients, and for production audio, the support for VST instruments and effects and ReWire give you all the tools you need to create stunning scores.

After completing this chapter, you should be able to do the following:

- Attach a video to a score
- Identify a basic tempo
- Mark hit points
- Fit the score to time
- Connect with VST instruments
- Add VST effects
- Connect to DAWs and other programs, using ReWire

Chapter 13
NOTION FOR iPAD

Notion for iPad is a powerful stand-alone app that is capable of producing serious notation projects. But it's even better as a companion to Notion 5. While not as full-featured as the desktop version, Notion for iPad includes many of the features that make Notion great, particularly its ease of use, excellent playback, and even a few things that are unique because of the multi-touch interface.

Notion for iPad will open any Notion file and display everything, even things it can't actually do. The Notion team says eventually the app will have all the features of the desktop program, and the recent version has taken many steps in that direction. Any Notion user who has an iPad will want the Notion app, too.

Most of the projects in this book can be completed using the iPad app, the exception being the NTempo/Live Performance project and the video scoring. You also cannot attach audio files.

Setup

Installation is automatic once you purchase the app from the App store. The app can be easily used by itself, but you can also connect a MIDI device via an iOS MIDI interface, the Camera Connection Kit, or even wirelessly through Bluetooth. These will be recognized automatically.

External iPad keyboards have limited functionality, as there are no keyboard shortcuts available in the app, but can be useful for typing lyrics and other text.

In-App Purchases

The sound set included with the app is fully functional but has a limited number of instruments. The full sound set or individual instruments can be purchased by clicking on the Notion Store button on the Startup Screen or in the Toolbar. Be careful about these as the files are quite large and will fill up 16 and 32 GB iPads pretty quickly.

> **⊘ TIP:** It's considerably cheaper to purchase bundles of expansion instruments rather than one at a time. If you are considering in-app purchases, look things over and see how many you are likely to need at one time or another and determine what the most cost-effective option is.

Interface

The interface for the app shares many characteristics with the desktop app and should feel fairly familiar, though there are also considerable differences due to the multi-touch interface of iOS. For detailed information on the interface, please consult the excellent online Help Guide.

Startup Screen

When you open the app, you'll see a startup screen listing all the available files and the option to create a new file or import one. Notion for iPad supports files from the desktop version, MusicXML files, MIDI files, and Guitar Pro TABs. Importing can be done through Dropbox, e-mail, iTunes, or the built-in browser.

Figure 13-1. The Notion for iPad Startup Screen.

Click Notion Store and select Download Scores to access the built-in web browser. The Feedback button also takes you to the browser but goes to the PreSonus website. There are some FAQs, links to the forum, and support along with the Feedback form. You'll find the Notion team to be very responsive, so don't hesitate to send in requests there or on the forum.

Getting Started

Let's look at one of the demo scores. Tap the Mozart Clarinet Concerto. Notion opens the score and you'll see the basic interface elements: the score, the palette, the virtual keyboard, and the Toolbar at the bottom. While not identical to Notion's interface, desktop users should find this has a familiar feel.

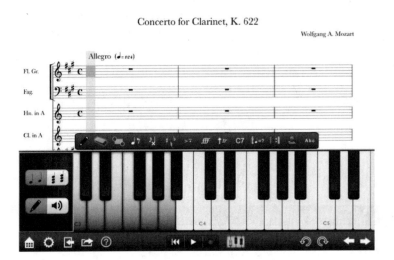

Figure 13-2. The main screen.

First, tap the Help [?] button in the Toolbar and select Quick Reference. You'll see that all of the basic interface elements are labeled. Tap anywhere on the screen to dismiss this and return to the score.

Tap the Instrument/Mixer toggle button twice so the keyboard is hidden. This provides a little more screen space for the score. Tap the Play button and listen to the really quite incredible playback. As it plays back, notice the details included and how it responds to articulations, dynamics, and the like, just as in the desktop version.

Toolbar

The Toolbar includes file-based menus, a transport, instrument and mixer buttons, Undo/Redo buttons, and Step Forward and Step Backward buttons.

The Home button will take you to the startup screen and close the current document.

The Gear menu displays View and Print options (printing requires an AirPrint printer on your network) and a link to Score Setup.

The Store menu links to the store and the browser.

The Export menu provides options to export to Dropbox, Notion, SoundCloud, and more.

Multi-touch Actions

Of course the biggest difference between the desktop and app versions is the multi-touch interface. There are no keyboard shortcuts in the app; everything is done by touch.

The *single tap* is the most commonly used action. Use it to operate the program, select items in the palette and place them in the score, and place the Edit marker in the score for playback and editing. The palettes are organized a little differently than in the desktop version, so tap each one and see where tools are located. The first two, the pencil and eraser, are single tools; the third palette also selects a measure. Technique palettes are contextual and will change depending on the instrument chosen.

The *double tap* is used to select a measure or item and display the context menu. You can accomplish the same thing by placing the cursor in a measure and tapping the Select icon in the palette.

Tap and hold on a measure displays the measure menu where you can define the bar, paste, and add multiple measures (insert barlines).

Tap and drag (tap and leave finger on screen while dragging) is used to create larger selections.

There are two actions to use for zooming. The common *two-finger pinch* in and out zooms in and out as it does on most iPad apps. The *two-finger double tap* toggles between fitting the width of the score to the screen and a smaller size. Experiment a little with the multi-touch actions.

> **! TIP:** Double-tapping a measure will also open the Selection palette.

Context Menus

Figure 13-3. The primary context menu.

The context menus play a much more important role in the app than in the desktop version, as this is the only way to access the included tools and commands. The main context menu is displayed when a measure is selected, either by double-tapping it or choosing the Selection box from the palette. The initial palette contains all the items you would expect in an Edit menu: Cut, Copy, Paste, Delete, and Selections.

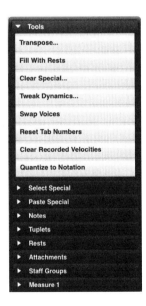

Figure 13-4. The secondary context menu.

In addition, there is a More button, which opens a second menu that bears close resemblance to the context menu in the desktop version. You'll want to take a look at each of the submenus, as these commands are available only through this menu.

Score Setup

Click the Home button and on the Startup screen, click New score to go to the Score Setup window. While it has most of the same functions as found in the desktop app, the interface is a bit different.

At the top, enter the title (required) and subtitle and composer, if desired. The instrument families are found on the right. Choosing one will display pictures of the available instruments along with instruments available as in-app purchases. Tap an instrument and it will be added to the score.

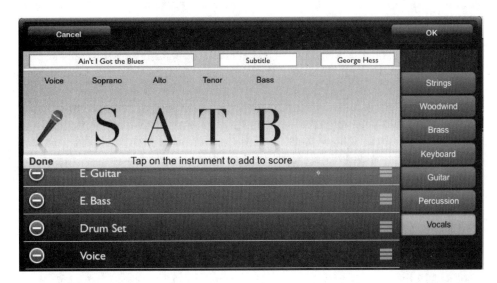

Figure 13-5. Editing Score Setup.

To move an instrument up or down: Tap the Edit button and drag the Move icon up or down.

To delete an instrument: Tap the Edit button and tap the red minus [–] symbol.

To hide an instrument (without deleting it): Tap the Eye icon.

Editing Instrument Properties

Tap the blue arrow to open the instrument setup window. In this window, you can choose the type of staff and transposition, change the instrument name, or choose another instrument entirely. For guitars and basses you can also set the tuning here.

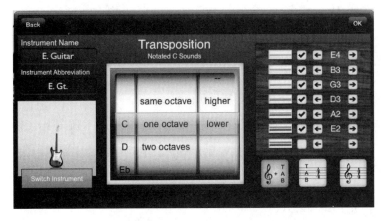

Figure 13-6. Instrument properties.

Note Entry

Just as in the desktop version of Notion, there are three basic ways to enter notes in the app: tap entry, step-time recording, and real-time recording. The most practical way is step-time recording, as it is faster than tapping and more accurate than real time. Because there are no shortcuts, editing is not as fast in the app as it is in the desktop version, so it's a good idea to minimize how much editing will be needed.

Real-time recording is essentially the same as in the desktop version (see Chapter 3). You will need an external MIDI keyboard or guitar. Place the Edit marker where you want to start, tap the Record button, and choose the recording options: metronome, count-in, minimum velocity and durations, tuplets, multi-voice, and MIDI instrument. Tap Start Recording and Play. Tap the Record button again to stop.

For Tap Entry, tap the pencil tool. The note palette opens automatically. Select the note value and tap in the score. You will want to zoom in to be able to accurately place the note.

Step-time recording, using one of the on-screen instruments, is very similar to tap entry. Select the keyboard or fretboard (the drumpad can is available only for drum staves). Tap either the Melody Mode or Chord Mode icon and the pencil. Tap the note value in the palette and tap a note or chord. Tap the advance arrow to move to the next step. If you make a mistake, tap Undo or tap the back arrow to highlight the note/chord and play the correct one.

Step-time recording with a MIDI keyboard or guitar is even faster. You can still use the advance and back arrows to place the Edit marker and correct mistakes. This is generally the most efficient method of note entry.

> **❶ TIP:** Ties across barlines cannot be entered during step-time recording as the Entry marker will have already moved to the next measure. Tap the Step Backward button, enter the tie, and tap Step Forward. Or just come back and add them after you've entered all the notes.

Note Editing

To change the pitch: Place the Edit marker over the note and play the correct note on the keyboard or fretboard. You can also tap and drag a note, but it's difficult to be accurate.

To change a note to a rest: Highlight the note and tap the appropriate rest.

To change a rest to a note: Highlight the rest and play a note on the keyboard.

To delete a note: Select the note (yellow) and tap the eraser.

To delete one note of a chord: Select the notehead and tap the eraser.

It will often be easiest to delete notes and re-enter them. The one exception is when only the pitch changes and the rhythm remains the same. To re-pitch an entire line, use an external MIDI device to advance automatically as in step-time. Set the first note you want to change and play. On some older iPads, you may have to go a little slower than you'd like. You can also re-pitch manually without a MIDI device, but you must tap the Step Forward arrow after each note.

Other Entries

One thing to be aware of is that for most items, you need to select the location in the score *before* selecting the item from the palette, the main exception being slurs. This is the opposite of most of the desktop methods, so be careful. It's very easy to start placing unintended things in the score.

Selections

As with Notion, there are three different types of selections.

The Blue selection selects measures or groups of notes.

The Green selection is the Edit/Entry marker.

The Yellow selection is the single-item selection.

> ❶**TIP:** Tap just below the staff to place the Edit marker.

Selecting a note (yellow) does not move the Edit marker (green). Some items, such as articulations and dynamics, will be placed on a selected note, rather than at the marker location. Other items, such as trills, will be placed at the marker's location. And still others will be placed at either.

Articulations and Dynamics

Articulations and dynamics work in a similar manner as in the desktop version. Articulations can be added to individual notes or contiguous groups. Dynamics are entered one at a time. Select one from the palette and click in the score.

Slurs can be found in the Articulation palette and the Selection palette and they work in distinct ways, though the result is the same. The slur in the Articulation palette works the same as the desktop version. Choose the slur, tap the first note, and then tap the last note of the phrase. Make sure the amber slur appears before tapping the ending note. The Slur tool in the Selection palette works a little differently. Here you select the notes to be included in the phrase first and then tap the Slur tool to place the slur. This works best when the phrase includes all notes in a measure or measures. Hairpins work in the same way.

> ❶**TIP:** If you need a slur to extend to a new line, Open iPad View Settings and reduce the notation size temporarily so that the notes you want to slur are all on the same line. Enter the slur as directed and then reset the score to the desired size.

Working on an iPad

If you are like the rest of us, you're spoiled from working on larger screens. But lest we forget, the original Macintosh had the same screen size as the iPad, but at a much lower resolution and on much slower computers. But we can still learn some useful things by remembering some of the tricks that made it possible to get things done.

View

The biggest challenge of working on an iPad is the small screen. This was also a big challenge on the early Macintosh. Some of the workarounds are:

- Use Continuous View for most tasks. Each staff is on its own line and it's easy to scroll left or right with a single finger swipe.
- Switch to Print View only when you are adjusting the layout for printing.
- Use Zoom In and Zoom Out. A lot. Unless you use a stylus, you will find it difficult to select items with your finger at normal size.
- For larger ensembles, hide staves and work in sections as much as possible.
- Reduce clutter. Hide the Entry Instruments/Mixer when not in use.

> **① TIP:** Using dynamic parts also makes editing easier. Edit any part and the edits appear in the score.

Workflow

In the desktop version, it's very easy to switch between tools or items, so you can pretty much work any way you like. But with no shortcuts on the iPad, those working in copyist mode may find it's faster to enter all items from a single palette and then move to the next one. For one, this will reduce the need to memorize the components of each palette. Composers, on the other hand, may choose to work differently. A major difference between the iPad app and the desktop is that step-time recording is done in Edit mode. This means that you can switch to any other palette anytime without leaving step-time recording.

Importing Files

One of the most useful features of the iPad app is its ability to import files. The built-in browser has links directly to some very useful sites for MusicXML, Standard MIDI, and Guitar Pro TAB files.

Importing a MusicXML File

- Open the app or tap the Home button.
- Tap the Notion Store button.
- Tap Download Scores.
- Scroll down to Download MusicXML.
- Tap Project Gutenberg.
- Tap Completed Scores.
- Tap Beethoven String Quartet No. 4 in C Minor.
- Tap the first XML version to download the score.
- Close the browser.
- Tap on the downloaded file in the score list.
- Tap Play.

You'll find that most dynamics, articulations, and phrasings play back correctly, but as in the desktop version the crescendos and decrescendos do not and will need to be replaced.

- Scroll to m. 11.
- Pinch and zoom in.
- Tap each hairpin and text "cresc." and tap the eraser.
- Two-finger double-tap to fit the width.
- Double-tap m. 11.
- Tap and hold the bottom handle and drag to the right through beat 1 of m. 13.
- Tap the crescendo hairpin.
- Repeat for the other three instruments.
- Set the cursor before the crescendo and tap Play.

All other items in the Selection palette work the same way. For example, in m. 34 a slur is missing on the grace notes into the first note in violin 2. Double-tap the measure. Tap and drag the bottom handle to the left so only the grace notes and first note are selected and tap the Slur tool in the palette.

Importing a Guitar Pro TAB File

Guitar Pro files are transcriptions of popular songs and solos made by Guitar Pro users. As such, they are subject to copyright laws and cannot be included in this book. However, they are available to use for individuals such as yourself. You will need a free account at www.guitarprotabs.org to download the files. At present, downloading TABs in the Notion browser does not work. However, it does work in Safari iOS, or you can download them on your computer and import them, using Dropbox or iTunes. Be forewarned: the files on this site will vary greatly in quality and accuracy.

- Open Safari on the iPad.
- Go to www.guitarprotabs.org.
- Log in.
- Search and select the TAB file of your choice.
- Tap the Download button.
- When the file appears, tap "Open in Notion."
- Open the file from the Notion Startup Screen.

Importing Files from Your Computer

You can use iTunes to transfer files from your computer to your iPad, but the Notion app provides a much easier solution. Support for Dropbox (www.dropbox.com), a free, cloud-based storage service, is built into the Notion app. You can save and open files directly in Dropbox from the Import and Export menus. Install the Dropbox app on your computer when you sign up for your account and get the Dropbox app for your iPad from the App store. Files will be stored in your Dropbox folder in the App folder under Notion Mobile.

Saving and Exporting Files

Files are saved automatically. You can also export them via e-mail or Dropbox. As with the desktop version, you can export directly to SoundCloud as a .wav or .aac file or export the file to disk as a MusicXML, Standard MIDI, or PDF file. Direct printing is supported through AirPrint.

Summary

Notion for iPad is a very powerful app, capable of doing real work, and it's a great companion to Notion 5. You can complete most of the projects in this book on the iPad, the exceptions being the chapters on live performance and video scoring.

Although the app handles all of the articulations, dynamics, and other entries, for scores, with a lot of detail work, I suggest exporting files to the desktop version to add articulations, dynamics, and phrasing, if possible.

Keys to Working in Notion for iPad

- Use Continuous View rather than Page or iPad view.
- Use screen sets. It's very easy to call up Score Setup and hide or show staves. Switch between note entry methods freely.
- Use Copy and Paste as much as possible.
- Re-pitching is faster than entering from scratch. Copy and Paste are even faster.
- A MIDI keyboard or guitar and interface is a very useful addition.
- For most entries, select the location first, then the item to be entered.
- Outside of multi-tapping rather than clicking, most items work in much the same way they do in the desktop version. The main exception is the items in the Selection method, which do not require a second click/tap.

AFTERWORD

By now, you realize that Notion isn't just a notation program. The combination of ease of use and great playback is unlike any other program. Those of you coming from another notation or DAW program will probably have developed some new ideas on how to work, and new users are already well on their way to being power users.

For support, there is a strong user base to be found on the PreSonus forum, http:// forums.presonus.com. You can find discussions for both Notion 5 and Notion for iPad. Notion has been around for a while, so many of the users here are very knowledgeable and very helpful. They were invaluable in providing quick answers for my questions. The Notion support team is also very helpful.

The future looks very bright for Notion. With the recent acquisition by PreSonus, Notion has entered a new era. It's clear that Notion is part of an overall strategy for the company for both professionals and educators. Notion 5 is the just the first step and it's clear we can expect more developments in the near future.

APPENDIX: ONLINE CONTENT

The supporting website is organized by chapter and includes all of the files you'll need to help you complete the projects in the book. The MusicXML, Standard MIDI, audio, and video files needed for each project can all be found there. The remaining files are there to support you as you work through each project. PDF files show music to be entered and the completed projects. Notion files are provided for those who would like to skip a few steps. The three videos demonstrate how I did the first project (in chapter 2). Finally, a demo version of the Sicilian Numerals font and a Max patcher that enables you to control NTempo using a MIDI footpedal are included.

Project Files and Examples

Chapter 2: Getting Started
major_scales.pdf—An example of the completed project

Chapter 3: Developing Your Workflow
entry_examples.pdf—Examples for note entry practice

Chapter 4: Songwriting
songwriting.notion—The completed project file

Chapter 5: The Lead Sheet
AintIGotTheBluesLS.pdf—An example of the completed project

Chapter 6: Guitar Techniques
blues_chart.pdf—An example of the completed project
blues_nosolo.notion—The completed chart, minus guitar solo
bluesLS.notion—The leadsheet
cadenza.wav—The transcribed cadenza as recorded
guitar_solo.notion—The solo transcribed
guitar_solo.wav—The transcribed solo as recorded

Chapter 7: Part Writing and Analysis
Chorale.pdf—An example of the completed project
bachchorale.xml—The MusicXML file for import

Chapter 8: The Ensemble Arrangement
Mozart_complete.pdf—An example of the completed project
WAM_Minuet.mid—The MIDI file for the project
Mozart_form.notion—The project, stage 1: Form only
Mozart_saxes.notion—The project, stage 2: Form and notes edited
Mozart_edited.notion—The project, stage 3: Pre-layout

Chapter 9: NTempo and Live Performance

MorningMood.xml—The MusicXML file for the project
MorningMood-edit.notion—Imported XML file
MorningMood-overlay.notion—The score, hairpins edited
MorningMood-perform.notion—The score, all edits completed

Chapter 10: Solo Piano

Chopin_Valse.pdf—The completed project
Valse-notes.notion—The project file, notes only

Chapter 11: The Jazz Ensemble

Way_Cool_Chart.pdf—The completed project
Way_Cool-form.notion—The score setup, no entries
Way_Cool_Bass_Line.pdf—The suggested bass line
Way_CoolLS.notion—Lead sheet without articulations
Way_Cool-articulations.pdf—Lead sheet with articulations
Way_Cool-articulations.notion—Lead sheet with hidden articulations
Way_Cool-horns.notion—Score with horns and bass only
Way_Cool-guitar.notion—Score with guitar entered (no drums)
Way_Cool-drums.notion—Score with playback drums entered
Way_Cool-intro.notion—Introduction and Coda (for copying)
riddimpiano.wav—Audio file for the solo section

Chapter 12: Scoring to Video

Yellowstone Morning SMPTE.mp4—Video file for the project

Video Demos for Project 1 (Chapter 2)

Project 1-Pt1.mp4—Project 1 video, part 1
Project 1-Pt2.mp4—Project 1 video, part 2
Project 1-Pt3.mp4—Project 1 video, part 3

Software

Sustain2C4.maxpat—Program for footpedal control of NTempo
SicilianNumeralsDemo.sit—Demo version of figured bass font

INDEX

quick PRO
guides *series*

Ableton Grooves
by Josh Bess
Softcover w/DVD-ROM •
978-1-4803-4574-4 • $19.99

Producing Music with Ableton Live 9
by Jake Perrine
Softcover w/DVD-ROM •
978-1-4803-5510-1 • $19.99

Sound Design, Mixing, and Mastering with Ableton Live 9
by Jake Perrine
Softcover w/DVD-ROM •
978-1-4803-5511-8 • $19.99

Mastering Auto-Tune
by Max Mobley
Softcover w/ DVD-ROM •
978-1-4768-1417-9 • $16.99

The Power in Cakewalk SONAR
by William Edstrom, Jr.
Softcover w/DVD-ROM •
978-1-4768-0601-3 • $16.99

Mixing and Mastering with Cubase
by Matthew Loel T. Hepworth
Softcover w/DVD-ROM •
978-1-4584-1367-3 • $16.99

The Power in Cubase
by Matthew Loel T. Hepworth
Softcover w/DVD-ROM •
978-1-4584-1366-6 • $16.99

Digital Performer for Engineers and Producers
by David E. Roberts
Softcover w/DVD-ROM •
978-1-4584-0224-0 • $16.99

The Power in Digital Performer
by David E. Roberts
Softcover w/DVD-ROM •
978-1-4768-1514-5 • $16.99

Electronic Dance Music Grooves
by Josh Bess
Softcover w/Online Media •
978-1-4803-9376-9 • $19.99

The iPad in the Music Studio
by Thomas Rudolph and Vincent Leonard
Softcover w/Online Media •
978-1-4803-4317-7 • $19.99

Musical iPad
by Thomas Rudolph and Vincent Leonard
Softcover w/DVD-ROM •
978-1-4803-4244-6 • $19.99

Live On Stage!: The Electronic Dance Music Performance Guide
by Josh Bess
Softcover w/Online Media •
978-1-4803-9377-6 • $19.99

Logic Pro for Recording Engineers and Producers
by Dot Bustelo
Softcover w/DVD-ROM •
978-1-4584-1420-5 • $16.99

The Power in Logic Pro
by Dot Bustelo
Softcover w/DVD-ROM •
978-1-4584-1419-9 • $16.99

Create Music with Notion
by George J. Hess
Softcover w/Online Media •
978-1-4803-9615-9 • $19.99

Mixing and Mastering with Pro Tools
by Glenn Lorbecki
Softcover w/DVD-ROM •
978-1-4584-0033-8 • $16.99

Mixing and Mastering with Pro Tools 11
by Glenn Lorbecki and Greg "Stryke" Chin
Softcover w/Online Media •
978-1-4803-5509-5 • $19.99

Producing Music with Pro Tools 11
by Glenn Lorbecki and Greg "Stryke" Chin
Softcover w/Online Media •
978-1-4803-5508-8 • $19.99

Tracking Instruments and Vocals with Pro Tools
by Glenn Lorbecki
Softcover w/DVD-ROM •
978-1-4584-0034-5 •$16.99

The Power in Reason
by Andrew Eisele
Softcover w/DVD-ROM •
978-1-4584-0228-8 • $16.99

Sound Design and Mixing in Reason
by Andrew Eisele
Softcover w/DVD-ROM •
978-1-4584-0229-5 • $16.99

Studio One for Engineers and Producers
by William Edstrom, Jr.
Softcover w/DVD-ROM •
978-1-4768-0602-0 • $16.99

HAL•LEONARD®
quickproguides.halleonardbooks.com
Prices, contents, and availability subject to change without notice.